Today's AI Artificial Intelligence

It's Not As Difficult As It Sounds!

By Maurice 'Big Mo', Chris & Killian Flynn

Let's Bring the Power of AI to Everyone!

Today's Simple AI™
TSAI

The FF Foundation is a not-for-profit,

AI research, development & teaching foundation,

currently funded by Open Doors Ltd.

TodaysSimpleAIForAll.eventbrite.com - *TodaysSimpleAI.com*

Any profits from this book will go to charity.
Published 2019 by The FF Foundation & Open Doors Ltd.
Images: Courtesy of Pixabay.com

About the Authors

Maurice "Big Mo" Flynn started using the **maths of today's AI at Cambridge University,** where he graduated top of his college in engineering, with a 1st in his thesis covering the probability of cracking. He has worked with big data throughout his career & has **advised thousands of companies, including Google & Facebook**. He has done extensive pro bono charity work and is a **best selling Amazon author and speaker** as well as a **RSA/IDM/CIM Fellow**.

Chris Flynn is an **author**, **copywriter** and **editor** with over **25 years** of experience in **international EFL publishing** and online **content creation**. He has a BA in Philosophy from the University of Warwick.

Killian Flynn is a natural mathematician and polyglot, who has taken his **data science thinking** into multiple fields **including physics, biology, agriculture, computer science plus politics and social planning**. He brings a usefully irreverent humour to this subject and also leads the **translation of the materials into multiple languages**.

Testimonials

"Extremely relevant & timely." Top Investment Bank

"Will use this on our AI courses." Top UK University

"Feel more confident about AI now." Ogilvy MD

"Now I really get it!" Google AI StartUp CFO

"Really useful for all our members." RSA

"Very clever approach!" Facebook VP

"Our industry must test this." PRCA

"We need this." WPP

Let's Bring the Power of AI to Everyone!

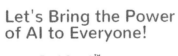

TODAY'S SIMPLE AI™

TSAI

Contents

Today's AI - Overview

What is Today's AI?

In general artificial intelligence means[1] software and machines that demonstrate equal or better than human effectiveness plus learning in complex challenges. There are two types of AI discussed today.

---

[1] https://en.wikipedia.org/wiki/Artificial_intelligence

What is Today's AI?

So called narrow AI[2] addresses single issues. This extends today from rich data analysis e.g. vision to content creation. General AI is more adaptable, like human intelligence. The expert consensus is that we are still far from this.

---

[2] https://hackernoon.com/general-vs-narrow-ai-3d0d02ef3e28

Why Is AI Exciting?

Around 2012 an approach called "deep learning[3]" was shown to enable rapid improvement in areas from computer vision to audio and text analysis and now even creation. This has caused excitement and fear.

---

[3] https://en.wikipedia.org/wiki/Deep_learning

Why Is AI Exciting?

The issue with deep learning is effectiveness is very high and has not been fully explained[4]. It therefore requires manual fiddling to work. A second approach called machine learning is much better understood has therefore been widely adopted.

---

[4] https://en.wikipedia.org/wiki/Deep_learning

How Does AI Work?

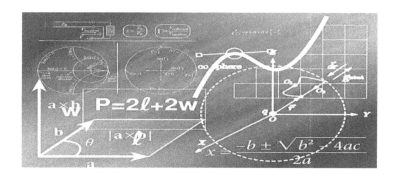

Today's AI[5] is a combination of old maths with new and ever cheaper computing power. It works via many computer languages.

[5] https://en.wikipedia.org/wiki/Deep_learning

How Does AI Work?

The process involves finding patterns[6] in historical data or content. These patterns can then predict future events, to understand images and even create content!

_____

[6] https://en.wikipedia.org/wiki/Deep_learning

What's Ethical AI[7]?

Ethical AI is a hot topic today. We need to make sure that we don't "bake" any bias into these systems. Of course the processes we use currently are far from unbiased.

---

[7]
https://www.lexology.com/library/detail.aspx?g=8a62e0af-8824-41a0-9602-9435b8a0f894

What's Ethical AI[8]

The AI solution to this involves ensuring data used is representative and used fairly, in line with any risks and with a people-first mindset. New privacy laws like GDPR can both help and hinder.

[8]
https://www.lexology.com/library/detail.aspx?g=8a62e0af-8824-41a0-9602-9435b8a0f894

What's Ethical AI[9]?

AI ethics questions to consider are:

"Is this a high-risk area needing extra care eg healthcare? Are we improving a biased system? Do we use data that is fair and representative? Are we aiming for some public good or solely private gain?"

The answers help guide us as to how fast we should go.

9

https://www.lexology.com/library/detail.aspx?g=8a62e0af-8824-41a0-9602-9435b8a0f894

Do I Need AI?

Well let's look to the near future.
Experts agree[10] AI will reach everywhere there is software. As a result we'll almost all need retraining plus need to battle AI misuse. Yet the potential benefits are huge.

---

[10]

https://www.weforum.org/agenda/2019/06/how-the-future-of-computing-can-make-or-break-the-ai-revolution/

Do I Need AI?

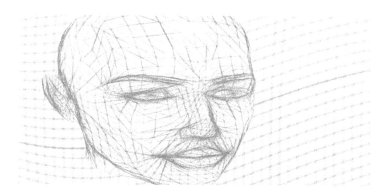

Here's a simple checklist we use:

"Do you have to make any important decisions based on "gut feel"? Do you sometimes fail to use customer data to continually improve? Do you have competition that is more savvy with data?" If you answered yes at all, do read on[11]!

11

https://www.weforum.org/agenda/2019/06/how-the-future-of-computing-can-make-or-break-the-ai-revolution/

Today's AI Challenges?

One issue that slows AI projects down is confusion about expertise needed. Too many experts in this space love the jargon[12] that makes this topic harder to understand.

---

[12]

https://www.techrepublic.com/article/mini-glossary-ai-terms-you-should-know/

Today's AI Challenges?

We have reviewed numerous AI case studies, tools & trainings. We calculate that 99% of the population need a simpler approach[13], in order to make AI accessible for all.

---

[13]

https://www.techrepublic.com/article/mini-glossary-ai-terms-you-should-know/

What's AI Good For?

Based on hundreds of case studies, research and our hands on work, thet top ethical opportunity we see is in enhancing our limited, human, expert resources via big data analysis and prediction as well as content processing and creation.

What's AI Good For?

The most excitement at the moment is probably in the following areas:

1. Automation e.g. admin, search, customer service, retail, logistics.

2. Prediction e.g. financial, HR, medical, security, marketing & sales.

3. Creation e.g. visual, aural, text.

Our AI Conclusions

Experts conclude AI can be a force for good[14] by putting expert capabilities in the hands of many more billions of people than ever before. Now we look at case studies showing how companies are doing that.

[14]

https://www.weforum.org/agenda/2019/06/how-the-future-of-computing-can-make-or-break-the-ai-revolution/

Today's AI - Case Studies

Case Study: Marketing & Creative

Adobe[15] **has been adding AI via machine learning** to their marketing and design tools to make these capabilities available to thousands of brands.

15

https://diginomica.com/2018/09/25/under-the-hood-of-adobe-sensei-how-ado be-is-evolving-their-analytics-with-ai/

Case Study: Marketing & Creative[16]

On the data side they are enabling real time personalization decisions. On the design side they are experimenting with adapting designs based on facial feedback, even using virtual reality face tracking tools!

[16]https://diginomica.com/2018/09/25/under-the-hood-of-adobe-sensei-how-adobe-is-evolving-their-analytics-with-ai/

Case Study: Marketing & Biz Dev[17]

M&C Saatchi posters read the expression on viewers' faces. AI tells if the response is positive or negative (smile/frown) and responds e.g. change colours, fonts, images et al, to turn a consumer's frown upside down.

---

[17]http://theconversation.com/now-advertising-billboards-can-read-your-emotions-and-thats-just-the-start-45519

Case Study: Marketing & Art[18]

In this example a robot has been built which uses today's AI software to which it to "see" the world around it and represent what it sees in paintings, which have sold for

---

[18] [VIDEO]: https://www.youtube.com/watch?v=8ozuZz8dU70

over £1m today. Is it art? The debate

rages!

Case Study: Marketing & Writing[19]

Alimama, the marketing mamma married to retail poppa Alibaba, uses AI copywriting software for product descriptions and simple ads for their sales platforms that they say pass the Turing test.

---

[19]https://www.adweek.com/digital/alibaba-says-its-ai-copywriting-tool-passed-the-turing-test/

Case Study: Marketing & Writing

While this is more a figure of speech to say it's intelligible and sounds natural (since no one's firing questions at it, as in the real Turing test), it can still pump out 20,000 lines of Chinese per second[20].

---

[20]https://www.adweek.com/digital/alibaba-says-its-ai-copywriting-tool-passed-the-turing-test/

Case Study: Marketing & Art[21]

Rutgers Art & AI Lab used AI tools (called GANs & CANs) to create original abstract artworks. They then threw in a bunch of works from Art Basel (created by real artists)

21 https://news.artnet.com/art-world/rutgers-artificial-intelligence-art-1019066

Case Study: Marketing & Art

and asked people to decide which were made by a human hand. GAN-CAN images fooled them 35% -53% of the time. Humans – must try harder![22].

---

[22] https://news.artnet.com/art-world/rutgers-artificial-intelligence-art-1019066

Case Study: Marketing & Writing[23]

"Did A Robot Write This?"

While robot writers still struggle with longer prose, they are getting quite good at short texts e.g. news headlines or email subject lines. In a recent example an AI digested 1 million news article and headline pairs

---

23

https://thenextweb.com/artificial-intelligence/2019/05/17/bad-news-journalists-robots-are-writing-really-good-headlines-now/

Case Study: Marketing & Writing[24]

> **HUMAN: 'Desperate search for Lebanon's mass graves'**
> **AI: 'The missing memories of Beirut'**

and mapped the patterns betwixt. It was then asked to generate new headlines for new articles and did well according to cynical hacks.

24

https://thenextweb.com/artificial-intelligence/2019/05/17/bad-news-journalists-robots-are-writing-really-good-headlines-now/

Case Study: Retail & Marketing[25]

Peter Glenn outdoors goods chain unleashed AI on their customer database & discovered over 80% of people hadn't visited for years. They re-engaged customers based on needs, likes & locations. As a result they boosted their AOV (Average Order Value) by 30%.

[25]https://emerj.com/ai-sector-overviews/5-business-intelligence-analytics-case -studies-across-industry/

Case Study: Retail & Marketing[26]

Starbucks launched a mobile app and rewards program that gives them enormous amounts of data from its 13 million users. It uses it to personalize the experience, so the customer can walk into a store

[26] https://bernardmarr.com/default.asp?contentID=1462

Case Study: Retail & Marketing[27]

anywhere and baristas will know what they drink at what time of day, what snacks they might enjoy, so they can suggest something new before the customer has even realized they were bored of their regular cup of joe.

Case Study: Retail & Marketing[28]

Coca Cola Amatil is the biggest distributor of soft drinks in the Asia Pacific region. With the help of Trax Retail Execution, with image-based AI they were able to track their product on the shelves in real time.

28

https://traxretail.com/wp-content/uploads/2015/08/TRE_Customer-Success.pdf

Case Study: Retail & Marketing

They spotted where and when there were shortfalls (or 'performance gaps', as they call them) and learning to anticipate them. As a result, they gained 1.3% of the market share, which is quite a few crates of cola[29].

---

[29]https://traxretail.com/wp-content/uploads/2015/08/TRE_Customer-Success.pdf

Case Study: Retail & Online

Amazon[30] **uses an AI engine to customize its recommendations**, which customers receive both onsite while shopping and by email. It is a measure of the success of this system that 30%

---

[30]http://rejoiner.com/resources/amazon-recommendations-secret-selling-onlin
e/

Case Study: Retail & Online[31]

of Amazon sales now come through its recommendations – and this before Alexa starts bullying you into getting her the latest surround sound music system.

---

[31]http://rejoiner.com/resources/amazon-recommendations-secret-selling-onlin e/

Case Study: Retail & Fashion[32]

Target app uses AI to find products to suit you. You're out & see an item you like, you take a pic and the app finds similar pieces from the Target repertoire for you to choose from. Impulse shopping for the 21st century.

---

[32]https://econsultancy.com/15-examples-of-artificial-intelligence-in-marketing/

Case Study: Retail & Sports[33]

Sport & retail brands looked for new opportunities in historic customer data. AI data analysis showed that many of their long held assumptions were incorrect. Changes delivered double digit growth.

[33] https://www.thejockeyclub.co.uk

Case Study: IT & Media

This non existent person[34] is created by setting 2 AI's against each other. One studies photos of faces and then creates what a face should look like. The 2nd judges the 'fake photo' against the real photos & rejects poor versions. The successes are published as non existent photos!

---

[34] Thispersondoesnotexist.com

Case Study: IT & Media[35]

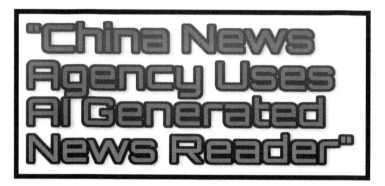

A Chinese news agency looking for news readers decided to use AI to generate them digitally! Thus fake news could be literally put into their digital mouths ... scary!

Case Study: IT & Social[36]

Wikipedia had such a problem with personal attacks that 40% of its volunteer editors had stopped contributing. Hard being a volunteer with feedback 'Your so rong & dum'. They used machine learning to teach a computer how to recognize abuse

---

[36] https://bernardmarr.com/default.asp?contentID=1549

Case Study: IT & Social[37]

and soon it could do so as well as human moderators. They then unleashed it upon 63 million comments to look for patterns. One discovery: 10% of abuse was coming from just 34 users.

---

[37] https://bernardmarr.com/default.asp?contentID=1549

Case Study: IT & Sales

MS and LinkedIn want the power of AI to be available[38] **to their millions of customers at the click of a button**. To that end they're building it into every tool from email to excel to LinkedIn recommendations and beyond.

---

[38] https://news.microsoft.com/features/democratizing-ai/

Case Study: IT & Sales

MS recognise that if it's not very simple to use then the majority won't.

Recent headlines: "AI tops LinkedIn fastest-growing job categories[39]"

"Microsoft's caricature AI turns photos into portrait cartoons[40]"

"MS Hummingbird is an AI powered news curator[41]"

[39]https://www.zdnet.com/article/artificial-intelligence-tops-linkedin-fastest-grow ing-job-categories/

[40]https://www.zdnet.com/article/how-microsofts-caricature-ai-turns-photos-into -portrait-cartoons/

[41]https://www.onmsft.com/news/microsoft-releases-hummingbird-an-ai-power ed-news-curator-for-android

Case Study: HR & Recruitment[42]

PWC, L'Oreal & Unilever all wanted to find new and better ways to help their teams recruit the best talent. An AI enhanced tool asked a series of questions to employees and

[42]https://www.pwc.at/de/publikationen/verschiedenes/artificial-intelligence-in-h r-a-no-brainer.pdf

Case Study: HR & Recruitment[43]

candidates. By analysing profiles of successful employees they were able to create a success model for recruitment as well as quantify its effectiveness in supporting HR.

---

[43]https://www.pwc.at/de/publikationen/verschiedenes/artificial-intelligence-in-h r-a-no-brainer.pdf

Case Study: Electronics & Social[44]

Samsung AI listens to online chat & carries out 'sentiment analysis', meaning the software finds out if people are saying good/bad things. They react to dissatisfaction fast e.g. they were getting negative buzz about a 'red tint' on S8 smartphone, so they kiboshed it.

---

[44]https://econsultancy.com/15-examples-of-artificial-intelligence-in-marketing/

Case Study: Electronics & Health[45]

Fitbit sells 14m units pa & that's a lot of heartbeats. Customers are a rich source of medical data. MS HealthVault allow patients to give their doctors access to their Fitbit data. John Hancock discounts health insurance if you share your data.

---

[45]https://www.reuters.com/article/us-manulife-financi-john-hancock-lifeins/strap-on-the-fitbit-john-hancock-to-sell-only-interactive-life-insurance-idUSKCN1LZ1WL

Case Study: Auto & Travel[46]

Tesla has AI in every car, gathering data and sending it into the cloud. Apart from the worth of this data, it has allowed Tesla cars to be trained in driver reaction,

---

[46]https://bernardmarr.com/default.asp?contentID=1251

Case Study: Auto & Travel[47]

road conditions and traffic behaviour, helping the vehicles hit the stage 2 autonomy they operate at today (i.e. car can drive itself in jams and on motorways). And soon they may be discussing the best way to get to Brighton on a bank holiday.

---

[47]https://bernardmarr.com/default.asp?contentID=1251

Case Study: Logistics & Online

AliBaba is known as the Amazon of China (although in China they probably call Amazon the AliBaba of the West). They used AI[48] to find the quickest and cheapest routes for

[48]https://www.zdnet.com/article/alibaba-wants-to-build-logistics-network-that-can-handle-1-billion-packages-a-day/

Case Study: Logistics & Online[49]

delivering worldwide. The result? **10% less vehicle use** & 30% less distance covered. With over 100 million packages being processed per day – and plans for a billion in future – that adds up to a chunk of change.

---

[49]https://www.zdnet.com/article/alibaba-wants-to-build-logistics-network-that-can-handle-1-billion-packages-a-day/

Case Study: Finance[50]

RBS utilizes AI to bring a more personal touch back to banking. Customers who contact the bank on their birthday may get a 'Happy birthday!' Customers paying twice for insurance can be informed of that. So if someone calls for your next birthday, it could be your bank manager!

---

[50] https://bernardmarr.com/default.asp?contentID=726

Case Study: Energy & Extraction[51]

Shell's exploratory drills cost big bucks but are hit and miss. They used to take 1000 readings before deciding, but with their new AI team, they analyse 1m+ increasing the chance of success. Hadoop crunched 46 petabytes of their data so far.

---

[51]https://bernardmarr.com/default.asp?contentID=688

Case Study: Energy & Smart City[52]

Milton Keynes is a new town and overpopulated. Using AI sensors, bins are emptied when full, lights turned off when no footfall and traffic lights adjusted, making the town fitter, leaner and with great abs. All software used is open source.

---

[52]http://www.energy-cities.eu/How-Milton-Keynes-used-artificial-intelligence-to-better-engage-with-its-5323

Case Study: Energy & Industry[53]

GE supplies 30% of the planet's electrical power & uses AI to predict when maintenance is needed, power demand peaks and create a networked model. Results 25% cut in operating costs; 5% cut in downtime.

---

[53]https://www.ge.com/research/technology-domains/artificial-intelligence

Case Study Conclusions[54]

Based on these case studies we conclude that use of AI stretches from proven to experimental. It makes sense that companies adopt a similar approach i.e. investment in relevant, proven use cases plus trial and testing for more experimental areas.

---

[54] https://todayssimpleai.com/blog/

Case Study Conclusions[55]

We also extrapolate from these case studies and our own experience to conclude the key success factors which distinguish between strong and weaker projects, which we do in the next section.

---

[55] https://todayssimpleai.com/blog/

Today's AI - Success Factors

Success Factors Intro[56]

Based on the previous case studies as well as our own extensive project work, we are now able to summarise the following success factors for AI projects i.e. common elements that seem to help deliver success.

---

[56] https://todayssimpleai.com/blog/

Success Factor 1: Simple Aims[57]

For many companies we find too much time is spent arguing about aims e.g. should we tackle a, b or c. The data experts then disappear for a week or so and more often than not come back saying the analysis can't be completed for many reasons.

---

[57] https://todayssimpleai.com/blog/

Success Factor 1: Simple Aims[58]

This is clearly inefficient so instead we have found it's better for the team together to dive into data or content processing as early as possible and let the best opportunities identified guide the priorities.

---

[58] https://todayssimpleai.com/blog/

Case Study: Review of Prototyping Tools[59]

Top AI Tool Review
https://todayssimpleai.com/blog

We review the top AI toolsets in the appendix & commend these, although not for newbies: Google Cloud Auto ML, Amazon Sagemaker, MS Automated ML.

---

[59] https://todayssimpleai.com/blog/

Case Study: Today's Simple AI™ Tools[60]

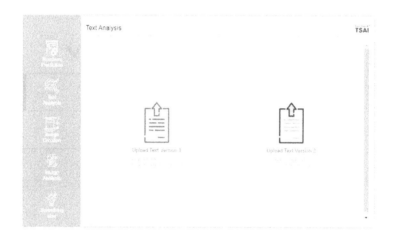

We also have created a web based toolset that all can easily use to start analysing data. Now used by a bank, university, ad giant, IT unicorn, major associations, schools & freelancers!

---

[60] https://TodaysSimpleAI.com

Success Factor 2 - Learning[61]

As with all new stuff it's important to help staff train themselves from top to bottom. Senior staff need to understand what the AI techniques can do and not do. Users of AI need to master data, tech and related skills.

---

[61] https://todayssimpleai.com/blog/

Success Factor 2 - Learning[62]

Other staff need to understand the project aims. We believe the best way is to embed "AI learn & play" in the business. We have reviewed most of the top AI training and learning programmes in the appendices.

Case Study: Review of AI Training[63]

Top AI Training Review
https://todayssimpleai.com/blog

We review the top AI trainings in the appendix & commend these, although not for non experts: Coursera AI Courses, Google Crash Course, Youtube Indies.

---

[63] https://todayssimpleai.com/blog/

Case Study: Today's Simple AI™ Tools[64]

Our Webinars

Today's Simple AI™
For Creative Content

Today's Simple AI™
For Creative People &
Projects

Today's Simple AI™
For Creative Results

Today's Simple AI™
For All

Hence we launched AI learning events that anyone can access and understand. Using these and similar we have taught thousands over the years and feedback is very positive!

---

[64] https://TodaysSimpleAI.com

Success Factor 3: Data & Content[65]

This is where many AI project shudder to a grinding halt. At best the data or content needed is scattered around in multiple formats, systems and silo's. At worst you don't know what you have or need. Do you want the good news?

---

[65] https://todayssimpleai.com/blog/

Success Factor 3: Data & Content[66]

We have some shortcuts. Firstly if someone has already built a similar AI model, you may be able to access and adapt & use it. If not some of the newest tools allow you to build your own model quite quickly without technical expertise.

---

[66] https://todayssimpleai.com/blog/

Success Factor 3: Data & Content[67]

Thirdly if you lack access to data internally, you can often find data online to use or scrape. After this low cost online teams can tidy up the data for fast use.

[67] https://todayssimpleai.com/blog/

Success Factor 3: Data & Content[68]

With the latest tools this data can be numbers, text, images or even audio and video files. E.g. Q: Can we find the best people to target? A: Yes here we can use historic and latest customer or employee data to find best groups of people to target.

---

[68] https://todayssimpleai.com/blog/

Success Factor 3: Data & Content[69]

Q: Can we become more visible for our brand strengths? A: Yes by analysing marketing data for effectiveness and creating more of the best content.

Q: Can we improve our business communication? A: Yes by analysing our comms and services data.

---

[69] https://todayssimpleai.com/blog/

Success Factor 3: Data & Content[70]

Gathering the data internally is usually an ad hoc process because data and content is often scattered across systems and in different formats. That's OK as the newest AI tools are designed to ingest lots of different data types and transform them into a usable format.

---

[70] https://todayssimpleai.com/blog/

Case Study: Free Datasets[71]

Let's Bring the Power
of AI to Everyone!

TODAY'S SIMPLE AI™
TSAI

By the time you read this, we should be live with our list and review of free datasets online which we can all use plus related tools. Using these we can massively boost our speed to launch by saving time on data collation and cleaning!

---

[71] https://TodaysSimpleAI.com

Success Factor 4: Choosing Tools[72]

Data can be uploaded into the AI tools manually or machine to machine. AI tools then turns the data into a format it can analyse and cycles the data through layers of analysis, correlating the relationships between data points. Each cycle gets better.

---

[72] https://todayssimpleai.com/blog/

Success Factor 4: Choosing Tools[73]

AI tools tell when the analysis is finished and tests the calculations using data that has been set aside. This "scores" its work to tell you how good it is. We see which customers are likely to buy, who should be recruited & which business content and comms works best.

---

[73] https://todayssimpleai.com/blog/

Success Factor 4: Choosing Tools[74]

The prototype stage for AI projects covers "train and test steps." This simply means we upload the data to our chosen system and ask it to find useful patterns e.g. correlations of activities vs. results or content vs. engagement or marketing vs. sales … and so on.

---

[74] https://todayssimpleai.com/blog/

Success Factor 4: Choosing Tools[75]

Fortunately new AI tools are emerging that aim to make the process simpler for all, with little or no specialist expertise needed. Here's the AI tool revolution we've seen:

---

[75] https://todayssimpleai.com/blog/

Success Factor 4: Choosing Tools[76]

Machine Learning tools launches:

1st Generation Tools: Needed technical and data experts. E.g. Google, MS, Amazon 2nd Generation Tools: Need only data expertise - launched in last 5 years. e.g. Google, MS, Amazon et al ML tools today. 3rd Generation Tools: Mostly need only general business expertise and willingness to learn. Launched in last year or two. Hooray! E.g. Driverless AI & Auto Machine Learning tools.

---

[76] https://todayssimpleai.com/blog/

Success Factor 4: Choosing Tools[77]

We always recommend the simplest to use, low-cost tools that anyone can use to get involved in the project without needing specialist tech or data know how. This allows the project stakeholders to get as close to the data analysis as possible, minimising delays.

---

[77] https://todayssimpleai.com/blog/

Success Factor 4: Choosing Tools[78]

Here are some of the best known tools which also usually offer free trials. We have a bigger list with detailed product reviews in the appendices.

- Google Cloud Auto ML
- Amazon Sagemaker
- MS Automated ML

---

[78] https://todayssimpleai.com/blog/

Case Study: **Today's Simple AI™** Tools[79]

We decided to create a set of tools which are easier and cheaper to use in order to bring the power of (deep learning) AI to more of the world's population, especially those lacking access to expertise, resources & budgets. All feedback welcome!

---

[79] https://TodaysSimpleAI.com

Success Factor 5: Using Tools[80]

We now consider if the project results look widely useful. If yes, then we may decide to use this "new system" on a regular basis & make it available to more people. To permit this, it needs a reliable, easy to use system and be updated regularly.

---

[80] https://todayssimpleai.com/blog/

Success Factor 5: Using Tools[81]

At roll-out stage we decide how much resources are worth investing in this approach. If the system improves on guesswork by 50% in a low-risk area then it sounds interesting for example. In higher risk areas, much more testing and benchmarking would be logical.

---

[81] https://todayssimpleai.com/blog/

Success Factor 5: Using Tools[82]

A recent change is the emergence of tools which allow you to learn and then scale up, all on the same platform. In the past the two stages were often separate, causing delays.

---

[82] https://todayssimpleai.com/blog/

Success Factor 5: Using Tools[83]

Sophisticated players may need to connect the AI system to an app or other experience, to drive that in real time. That's done through a connection gateway called an API.

Success Factor 5: Using Tools[84]

For many businesses in our experience, what's more useful is a no-code, self updating toolset where marketers and colleagues can play with data and content to find these new and useful business patterns and correlations.

---

[84] https://todayssimpleai.com/blog/

Success Factor 5: Using Tools[85]

One of the issues with most of the toolsets we review here, is that although they have done a good job in removing the tech requirements (i.e. no coding needed), most still do require a fair bit of data science confidence. Fortunately there are a few exceptions - see appendices.

[85] https://todayssimpleai.com/blog/

Case Study: Review of Enterprise Tools[86]

We review the top AI toolsets in the appendix & commend these, although not for newbies: Google Cloud Auto ML, Amazon Sagemaker, MS Automated ML.

---

[86] https://todayssimpleai.com/blog/

Case Study: Today's Simple AI™ Tools[87]

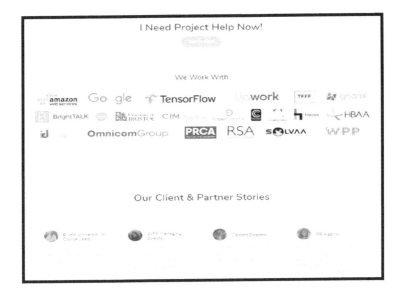

We built our own toolset on the back of an enterprise ready system (Tensorflow) hence we know it scales as needed. It's available to all.

Our AI Conclusions: Let's Play & Learn

Let's Bring the Power of AI to Everyone!

TODAY'S SIMPLE AI™

TSAI

In summary we recommend:

1.Quickly agree with project stakeholders areas possibly worth exploring. 2.Gather data or content that's easily available and start with that. 3.Start with AI tools that don't require specialist knowledge, so everyone is involved and fast! 4.Keep playing, learning and celebrating success!

Appendix 1 - Our Reviews of AI Toolsets

1.1 Wipro Holmes

What is Wipro Holmes? Wipro Holmes is an AI platform offering companies the ability to automate many parts of their operation, from data analysis and language processing to drone and robot management. How cool does that sound?! **Is Wipro Holmes for experts or beginners? Wipro Holmes** is intended to be used by the everyman, though there is scope for fine-tuning by experts. **Is Wipro Holmes for big companies or small? Wipro Holmes'** name was clearly inspired by IBM Watson, and on that basis we can assume it is pitching itself towards the smarter, leaner end of the market. **Is Wipro Holmes expensive?** With a quote-based plan and no free trial, we can assume **Wipro Holmes'** services do not come particularly cheap. **What are the benefits of Wipro Holmes? Wipro Holmes** boasts the AI abilities of voice recognition, language processing, pattern-recognition, prediction and hypothesizing. **Wipro Holmes** is easy to instruct and easy to access. **Wipro Holmes** can be used to control your robots and your drones - which sounds great, but how many companies really need this service yet? **What is Wipro Holmes not so good at?** The worry is that, despite his name, **Wipro Holmes** still cannot really do as much as his plumper sidekick. **How popular is Wipro Holmes?** Users give **Wipro Holmes** a score of 80% for user satisfaction in independent web research. **What equipment is needed for**

Wipro Holmes? Wipro Holmes works on Windows and Mac and web-based devices.

1.2 Apache PredictionIO

What is Apache PredictionIO? **Apache PredictionIO** is the open-source platform that allows rebel users to build their own machine learning engines to launch at the web. **Is Apache PredictionIO for experts or beginners?** Open source always has a tendency to frighten the uninitiated, who expect to see something like the lines from The Matrix when they boot up the system. It shouldn't be this way, since it is far more approachable, but the truth that many open-source enthusiasts won't admit is that users do need to know their way around a computer (and back). **Is Apache PredictionIO for big companies or small?** Just as IBM and big companies go together, so with **Apache PredictionIO** and the small. Not that it can't allow you to grow into a very large pair of boots (or make you look like you wear a very large pair) – just that smaller tend to be more open to open source in our experience. **Is Apache PredictionIO expensive? Apache PredictionIO**, like everything else from the Apache Software Foundation, is free. That's why they're Apache. Of course then set up and integration costs need to be added on top. **What are the benefits of Apache PredictionIO?** First of all, **Apache Prediction** is free. That's an important first of all. Second, **Apache PredictionIO** can be used with a whole swathe of other open source software, from Apache Spark to MLlib, HBase, Elasticsearch and more. **Apache PredictionIO** also has a templates library available, allowing users to pick and adapt the one that best suits their needs, saving them time and headaches. **Apache PredictionIO** has both web and mobile API applicability. **What is Apache PredictionIO not so good at?** For inexperienced users, there's a steep learning curve, which means it might not be ideal for companies trying to train up staff (in the sense that you're training them for their next job, in a new field altogether :-). **How popular is Apache PredictionIO?** Independent research has given 100% user satisfaction feedback with **Apache PredictionIO**. While it is a given that only open source enthusiasts use it, and therefore there is a pre-existing bias, still: if there was a problem, that also means you'd hear about it. **What equipment is needed for Apache PredictionIO?** Once set up **Apache PredictionIO** can works on Windows, Mac and, inevitably, Linux. It also works for web and mobile applications. However it isn't ready to go nor plug and play.

1.3 IBM Watson

What is IBM Watson? IBM Watson is the complete package. It will wine you, dine you and then, probably, reassign you (to a department more suited to your needs). It provides complete control over not only data flow but also intellectual property, human resources and much much more. It intends, in fact, to be the only platform you will ever need. **Is IBM Watson for experts**

103

or beginners? **IBM Watson** is definitely not for beginners, and with a fairly long training curve (though the training given is itself regarded as good). **Is IBM Watson for big companies or small? IBM Watson** unashamedly pitches itself toward large companies, institutes, hospitals and local and national governments, if not intergalactic alliances (as yet). **Is IBM Watson expensive?** In the pricing we can again see what kind of customer would suit **IBM Watson** (the software decides if you are worthy). For $30 a month, a single user gets 2 GB of storage; for $80, an unlimited number of users can share out 100GB. **What are the benefits of IBM Watson? IBM Watson** knows what it's doing. If you are a big organisation – or on your way to becoming one – then IBM Watson will have anticipated most if not all of your needs. From personnel needs to bots to answer everyday queries, and from equipment shortages to near real-time reaction to events, this platform will do it all. **What** is **IBM Watson not so good at?** Again, fairly predictably, flexibility and individualization are not **IBM Watson**'s strong points. Another complaint is the training time, which means new employees can't jump onboard quite so quickly, and ex-employees' absence is more felt. **How popular** is **IBM Watson?** 99% user satisfaction returned by independent research gives a good indication of how well the software performs, though in many cases it would be preaching to the converted. **What equipment is needed for IBM Watson?** The **IBM Watson** software works well with Windows, Mac and Linux, as well as browser- based devices.

1.4 Google Cloud Machine Learning Engine

What is Google Cloud Machine Learning Engine? Google Cloud Machine Learning Engine is a cloud-based modelling platform for predictive analysis from Google. It can be used for small or large data groups. Users can create prediction models and scale up as large as needed. Already-made models can be imported, used and shared too. **Is Google Cloud Machine Learning Engine for experts or beginners?** While not for absolute beginners, the scalability does allow you to start small and then ramp up, and Google users will find it follows the Google mindset. **Is Google Cloud Machine Learning Engine for big companies or small? Google Cloud Machine Learning Engine** is built to appeal to a wide range of users including small business, large enterprises, medium sized Businesses and even freelancers. **Is Google Cloud Machine Learning Engine expensive?** There's a free and a paid version, of course, with a free trial of 1 month on the paid. If you go for the paid, you can choose to aim for just the US, Europe or Asia, or any combination thereof, which can cut down the cost. Specifically training a prediction models starts from US$0.49/hour and running a prediction model on going starts from $0.10/thousand predictions + $0.40/hour. **What are the benefits of Google Cloud Machine Learning Engine? Google Cloud ML Engine** offers scalable machine learning so users can design prediction models using large data sets which can then be used by many people across the world. **Google Cloud ML Engine** is well integrated so it links seamlessly with other Google services and platforms. For example you'll find it easy to couple it up with Google BigQuery and Google Cloud Dataflow, among others. Big storage, great customer support and plenty of guidance are often mentioned in customer reviews online. **Google Cloud Machine Learning Engine** uses Hypertune, which is a tool that automates models training. This enables users to see results faster vis semi-automation. **Google's Cloud Machine Learning Engine** has deep learning capabilities which means it uses the latest techniques and enables big and messy data usage. **What is Google Cloud Machine Learning Engine not so good at?** Like many of the tools in this space, **Google Cloud Machine Learning Engine** requires technical and data science expertise to master which many companies lack still. The fact that it is cloud based is always going to be a disadvantage for some users. **How popular is Google Cloud Machine Learning Engine?** Independent research has shown that 90% of users express satisfaction with **Google Cloud Machine Learning Engine**. Social media buzz also appears more positive than negative. **What equipment is needed for Google Cloud Machine Learning Engine**? As its cloud based, local set-up requirements for **Google Cloud Machine Learning Engine** are minimized. It works on Windows, Mac and browser based devices.

1.5 Azure Machine Learning Studio

What is Azure Machine Learning Studio? Azure Machine Learning Studio is a set of tools from Microsoft which allows the user to create ML models quickly and adapt them easily. Drag-and-drop format makes creating, changing, running and publishing experiments almost child's play. However some basic statistics know-how is helpful. **Is Azure Machine Learning Studio for experts, intermediates or beginners?** The drag-and-drop format where available means **Azure Machine Learning Studio** is highly intuitive, allowing the beginner to intermediate to start creating almost from day one. The fact that it is made by Microsoft means that a large number of users will find its interfaces somewhat familiar. However it does require statistics knowledge not least in terms of jargon. **Is Azure Machine Learning Studio for big companies or small? Azure Machine Learning Studio** is meant to appeal to a wide range of users, especially considering its easy-access and usability. However the pricing model (see below) might make it less attractive to large enterprises with huge data requirements as costs would mount. **Is Azure Machine Learning Studio expensive?** Users will quickly find the free version of **Azure Machine Learning Studio** limiting, but it's a great place to try things out. The paid version costs $9.99 per month, but that's per seat, so the cost could rise rapidly if your company has multiple users. And at $1 per studio experimentation hour, things could add up fast that end too. (Prices correct at time of review.) **What are the benefits of Azure Machine Learning Studio?** Part of the attraction of **Azure Machine Learning Studio** is – dare we say it – that it's almost fun to use, which makes it very accessible. You can go from newbie to pushing models online within the space of a few hours, too, and that always feels good. **What is Azure Machine Learning Studio not so good at?** Two common complaints seen online with **Azure Machine Learning Studio** are the speed of returning results and the level of support. The cost is also somewhat off-putting to some. **How popular is Azure Machine Learning Studio?** Online research gives a 97% user satisfaction with **Azure Machine Learning Studio**, which gives you a good idea of how user-friendly its interface and set-up really are.

What equipment is needed for Azure Machine Learning Studio? Azure Machine Learning Studio has a web interface so works on Windows and Mac, but as a Windows product, it makes the most sense in the Microsoft universe.

1.6 Google TensorFlow

What is TensorFlow? **TensorFlow** is the open-source library of AI software that was first developed by Google Brain for internal use before being made available to everyone. **Is TensorFlow for experts or beginners?** **TensorFlow** has a great deal of flexibility and adaptability, but it can in no way be called easy to use. **Is TensorFlow for big companies or small?** **TensorFlow** allows small companies to compete with the big boys in terms of creating powerful analytical engines. Big companies can by all means use it, but may find they want something a bit more ready made. The GPU is where it thrives, but it will function perfectly well on a CPU, allowing very small operations to apply it. **Is TensorFlow expensive? TensorFlow** is completely free, and its library is being added to all the time. **What are the benefits of TensorFlow?** As mentioned above, **TensorFlow** is free. Second, **TensorFlow** is the big daddy of AI software, being what Google developed and uses, and if Google uses it, we know it works. Since it went open-source, enthusiasts worldwide have been adding to the platform. **TensorFlow**'s recent eager execution innovation allows simple fast debugging. **TensorFlow** has mobile API applicability, making it ideal for those working on the hop. **TensorFlow** manages tasks like translation, place identification from photographs and voice recognition with ease. **What is TensorFlow not so good at?** For inexperienced users, it can be off-putting in terms of set-up and operation. **How popular is TensorFlow?** Independent research has given 99% user satisfaction feedback with**TensorFlow**. **What equipment is needed for TensorFlow? TensorFlow** works on Windows, Mac and Linux. It also works for mobile devices including (somewhat unsurprisingly) Android.

1.7 Ayasdi

What is Ayasdi? **Ayasdi** is a platform containing all the apps, tools and technologies users need to create a custom AI system, whether small scale or enterprise size. **Is Ayasdi for experts or beginners?** While not entirely for beginners, **Ayasdi** has been specifically designed to help businesses with their particular needs and issues, so that users from this area will find it has anticipated many of their problems. **Is Ayasdi for big companies or small? Ayasdi** can do small, but the bigger an enterprise gets, the happier this animal seems. **Is Ayasdi expensive?** Unusually, **Ayasdi** does not offer a free trial, and asks interested parties to get in contact for a quote. That means expensive, as a rule. **What are the benefits of Ayasdi? Ayasdi** automatically categorizes and finds patterns in data, then predicts and acts upon them. The extra intelligence function that it has is the ability to justify its ideas, making it near-unique in the market and, frankly, pretty close to getting one up on Turing. **Ayasdi** has the advantage of having been designed for enterprises, meaning it can easily be deployed company-wide, where it can fulfil even the day-to-day needs such as single sign-on. This means it can act as an operational system if desired, and not just an analytic machine. **What is Ayasdi not so good at? Ayasdi** is not best suited for the pure crunching of enormous amounts of data – for example, Hadoop data. It needs be fed more organised sets. **How popular is Ayasdi?** Though **Ayasdi**, as mentioned above, may be expensive, it seems to be worth it for those users who *did* dig into their pockets, as they have recorded 100% satisfaction in online reviews. **What equipment is needed for Ayasdi? Ayasdi** works on Windows, Mac, Linux and browser-based devices.

1.8 Infosys Nia

What is Infosys Nia? Infosys Nia is an AI platform that is one of the children of the Infosys AiKiDo family. It aims to take the pain out of the day-to-day processes an organization needs to perform, as well as assist it in innovating and improving its performance. **Is Infosys Nia for experts or beginners? Infosys Nia** makes a good attempt to simplify the complex and the vast, and even to make the experience of the user and enjoyable one, so beginners will definitely give it points for trying. **Is Infosys Nia for big companies or small? Infosys Nia** can scale both ways, but it's big talents might be lost on very small-size enterprises. **Is Infosys Nia expensive? Infosys Nia** will give you a quote if you contact them, and there is no free trial, which generally smells of money. They do emphasize that the cost to benefits equation stacks heavily towards the latter. **What are the benefits of Infosys Nia? Infosys Nia** will take all the mundane but necessary jobs out of the hands of people, freeing them up for more creative work. **Infosys Nia** provides valuable assistance in how to utilize its talents to the optimum, and provides suggestions on extending its use that clients had not thought of before.

Infosys Nia offers fast, flexible and efficient processing of big data. **What is Infosys Nia not so good at? Infosys Nia** is good at the big stuff, and understands what every company needs, but it's not so easy to individualize, so niche enterprises might not have their needs met. **How popular is Infosys Nia?** Web-based research gives **Infosys Nia** an 80% satisfaction score from users. **What equipment is needed for Infosys Nia? Infosys Nia** works on Windows, Mac and web-based devices.

1.9 Meya

What is Meya? **Meya** is a software platform specializing in the deployment of bots to aid with customer services and sales support. **Is Meya for experts or beginners? Meya** is custom-made for businesses to implement fast and easy. They boast that they deal with the technical side, leaving sales and other department to set the bots to work on exactly what they want them to do speedily and hitchlessly. **Is Meya for big companies or small? Meya** operates on a quote by quote pricing model, and seems confident that it can meet the needs of small through medium right up to transformer-sized enterprises.**Is Meya expensive?** Contact **Meya** for a price plan, though we can practically guarantee it will leave your wallet a lot lighter. **What are the benefits of Meya? Meya** takes the pressure off sales support and customer service, taking over the humdrum repetitive tasks and giving the human staff more time to spend on the quality interactions. **Meya** allows sales departments to operate better with fewer staff by AI interactions. **Meya** encourages teamwork by allowing multiple user access to its cloud platform. **Meya** integrates well with analytics platforms like Google Analytics. **What is Meya not so good at? Meya** is cloud based, which makes the user rather dependent on the host. Some people like this less than others. **How popular is Meya?** Users give **Meya** a score of 95% for user satisfaction in independent research. **What equipment is needed for Meya? Meya** works on Windows and Mac. It is a cloud-based service.

1.10 Nvidia Deep Learning

What is Nvidia Deep Learning? The **Nvidia Deep Learning** machine intelligence product suite gives the user the analytics it needs to crunch big data, making predictions and finding solutions. **Is Nvidia Deep Learning for experts or beginners? Nvidia Deep Learning** wants to be the everyman of AI, and to this end it does make an effort to be somewhat more accessible to beginners. **Is Nvidia Deep Learning for big companies or small? Nvidia Deep Learning** says it can work on a small scale, but since its target customers range from industry leaders to medical institutions and governments, we can make the inference that it's happiest with the big boys. **Is Nvidia Deep Learning expensive?** With no free trial, and prices individually tailored to the customer, it's safe to assume **Nvidia Deep Learning** is expensive. **What are the benefits of Ayasdi? Nvidia Deep**

Learning incorporates AI in security, allowing users to feel safe in the knowledge that it is learning about threats in something close to real time.**Nvidia Deep Learning** training courses are well-regarded by people within the industry and outside. **Nvidia Deep Learning** is used by many scientists, doctors, researchers and governments to digest the huge quantities of data they produce. **Nvidia's** involvement with hardware could prove attractive to customers who prefer all-in-one suppliers. **What is Nvidia Deep Learning not so good at?** Being more interested in the bigger picture, **Nvidia Deep Learning** might not be ideal when looking for individualized, highly customized solutions. **How popular is Nvidia Deep Learning? Nvidia Deep Learning** gets 99% user satisfaction in online reviews. **What equipment is needed for Nvidia Deep Learning? Nvidia Deep Learning** works on Windows, Mac, Linux and browser-based devices.

1.11 Rainbird

What is Rainbird? Rainbird is an AI platform for decision-making and solution-producing that has won awards. **Is Rainbird for experts or beginners? Rainbird** has an extremely user-friendly interface, allowing those with little knowledge of code to dive right in. **Is Rainbird for big companies or small? Rainbird** is designed to take over from the thousands of day-to-day decisions that clog up an organization's desk, and on that basis it is aimed towards mid- to plus-size businesses – or at least would be of most benefit to them. **Is Rainbird expensive? Rainbird** is quote based and provides no opportunity for a free trial, so contact the vendor, telling your eyes to be prepared to water. **What are the benefits of Rainbird? Rainbird** is very intuitive, with users working on the Rainbird Authoring Platform creating a Knowledge Map while the Rainbird Cognitive Reasoning Engine rumbles along underneath, do the heavy lifting. **Rainbird** can run a number of complex, data-dense operations at the same time. **Rainbird** used RBLang, an easy-to-grasp language that beginners can ease into. **Rainbird**'s Knowledge Maps offer simple integration into other systems by virtue of **Rainbird**'s open architecture. **What is Rainbird not so good at? Rainbird** does something quite specific, and enterprises might find they need to invest in another software package to have all their needs fulfilled. **How popular is Rainbird?** Web research gives **Rainbird** a score of 96% for user satisfaction. **What equipment is needed for Rainbird? Rainbird** works on Windows, Mac and web-based devices.

1.12 Receptiviti

What is Receptiviti? **Receptiviti** is an AI software platform that offers companies and organizations a way to analyze and understand both their staff and their client base better. **Is Receptiviti for experts or beginners? Receptiviti** has a number of large concepts to grapple with, but this shouldn't prove too much of an obstacle to the computer-savvy beginner. **Is Receptiviti**

115

for big companies or small? **Receptiviti** is confident it can help anyone, from enterprises run by less than 50 people to companies with over 1000. **Is Receptiviti expensive?** There's no free trial, and the company will give you a quote when you contact them, so paying for **Receptiviti** may hurt a little. **What are the benefits of Receptiviti? Receptiviti**'s patented software can analyze both personnel and customer psychology, giving a company unique insights and allowing predictive and proactive behaviour. **Receptiviti** can help HR find the right people for vacancies and analyze employee satisfaction, emotional state and both mental and physical fitness. It might even find your perfect match. **Receptiviti** is designed to spot problems before they develop and act to head them off. **What is Receptiviti not so good at? Receptiviti** does one thing very well, but you might have to fork out for another AI platform to do the other stuff. **How popular is Receptiviti?** Independent research gives **Receptiviti** a perfect user satisfaction score of 100. **What equipment is needed for Receptiviti? Receptiviti** works on Windows, Mac and web-based devices.

1.13 Salesforce Einstein

What is Salesforce Einstein? **Salesforce Einstein** is a software application designed to consume and digest great quantities of sales data. It allows sales teams access to the kind of hard processing they've previously only dreamed of, and provide them with predictions, suggestions and solutions. **Is**

Salesforce Einstein for experts or beginners? Salesforce Einstein is aimed at the beginner, and not only that: it is designed to be completely accessible to sales reps who do not want their time taken up with learning new software. **Is Salesforce Einstein for big companies or small?** As **Salesforce Einstein** is aimed at the sales department rather than the entire company, it is safe to assume that their pitch is towards the whale end of the scale rather than the feisty minnow. **Is Salesforce Einstein expensive? Salesforce Einstein** offers a free trial, as with all comparable software, but unusually it does not quote a price for the full version: it asks to be approached for a quote. In our experience, that means the product being hawked is not expensive – it's *very* expensive. **What are the benefits of Salesforce Einstein? Salesforce Einstein** will coordinate and help organize a sales team, taking over a lot of the drudge of calendaring and identifying potential contacts, enabling the team to get on with doing what it does best - selling. **Salesforce Einstein** crunches massive amounts of sales data to make market predictions and anticipate customer needs. **Salesforce Einstein** also has the AI bot-ability to provide ground-level sales support. **What is Salesforce Einstein not so good at? Salesforce Einstein** is somewhat narrow in scope, which could be good or bad depending on where you're coming from. So from a sales department in a large enterprise, it's a resounding cheer, where for anyone looking for something with a wider or more general scope, it's a big fat boo. **How popular is Salesforce Einstein?** Independent research tells us that **Salesforce Einstein** satisfies 96% of users (the other 4% are presumably the ones in charge of the sales department budget). **What equipment is needed for Salesforce Einstein? Salesforce Einstein** works on Windows, Mac and browser-based devices. It's worth pointing out that it's supported in English, Dutch and Swedish rather than just the usual English – though the extra language choices do seem a touch eclectic.

1.14 Today's Simple AI™

What is Today's Simple AI™? Today's Simple AI™ is an easy to use toolset which aims to bring the power of AI i.e. data analysis, prediction and content generation, to people everywhere even when lacking in expertise or resources. **Is Today's Simple AI™ for experts or beginners?** Today's Simple AI™ is used by beginners to experts due to its ease of use and low costs. It's probably most attractive to the less experienced and under resourced. **Is Today's Simple AI™ for big companies or small?** Today's Simple AI™ can be used by companies of all sizes. It's probably most relevant to those with less resources in this area. **Is Today's Simple AI™ expensive? Today's Simple AI™** is free to use for all the core tools on the website. We have a charity arm for pro bono projects and a Ltd. company for commercial projects.**What are the benefits of Today's Simple AI™?** **Today's Simple AI™** has the benefits of being free to use on the website, easy to use even for non experts and keeps data local and private as much as possible. **What is Today's Simple AI™ not so good at? Today's Simple AI™ is tailored for new, younger, less resourced projects. If you are an AI expert you may find it over simplifies the processes. How popular is Today's Simple AI™?** It's early days but feedback so far has been very positive. **What equipment is needed for Today's Simple AI™? Today's Simple AI™** works on PC, Mac and mobile devices.

Appendix 2 - AI Training Courses Reviewed

2.1 Today's Simple AI™ Training

What is Today's Simple AI™ training? **Today's Simple AI™** training is an easy to understand training course which aims to bring the power of AI i.e. data analysis, prediction and content generation, to people everywhere even when lacking in expertise or resources.

Is Today's Simple AI™ training for experts or beginners? **Today's Simple AI™ training** is used by beginners to experts due to it's ease of use and low costs. It's probably most attractive to the less experienced and under resourced.

Is Today's Simple AI™ training for big companies or small? **Today's Simple AI™** training is used by companies of all sizes. It's probably most relevant to those with less resources in this area.

Is Today's Simple AI™ expensive? **Today's Simple AI™** is free to use for all the core tools on the website. We have a charity arm for pro bono projects and a Ltd. company for commercial projects.

What are the benefits of Today's Simple AI™? **Today's Simple AI™** has the benefits of being free to use on the website, easy to use even for non experts and keeps data local and private as much as possible.

What is Today's Simple AI™ not so good at? Today's Simple AI™ is tailored for new, younger, less resourced projects. If you are an AI expert you may find it over simplifies the processes.

How popular is Today's Simple AI™? It's early days but feedback so far has been very positive.

What equipment is needed for Today's Simple AI™? Today's Simple AI™ works on PC, Mac and mobile devices.

2.2 Udacity Machine Learning Engineer Nanodegree

What is Udacity Machine Learning Engineer Nanodegree? Udacity Machine Learning Engineer Nanodegree (apart from being quite a mouthful) is an online course for learning to create predictive models and use decision-making algorithms, which lasts for six months and comes from the Kaggle team of educators.

Is Udacity Machine Learning Engineer Nanodegree for experts or beginners? Udacity Machine Learning Engineer Nanodegree boasts that it can take the novice to knowledgeable in half a year.

Is Udacity Machine Learning Engineer Nanodegree expensive? Udacity Machine Learning Engineer Nanodegree offers a free trial of 7 days, then charges £150 sterling per month, for a grand total of £900 – which is certainly not chickenfeed.

What are the benefits of Udacity Machine Learning Engineer Nanodegree? Udacity Machine Learning Engineer Nanodegree will take the user through nine separate projects, allowing practical and results oriented application from day one. **Udacity Machine Learning Engineer Nanodegree** takes users through models from a smartcab simulation to image classification. **Udacity Machine Learning Engineer Nanodegree** teaches through reinforcement. There are many other courses on offer on the **Udacity** platform, meaning learners who enjoy the method of training can take more.

What is Udacity Machine Learning Engineer Nanodegree not so good at? The last two months of the course teach about preparing your CV and preparing for an interview (with its inevitable assessment component). This may not be of any interest to some learners.

How popular is Udacity Machine Learning Engineer Nanodegree? It's been around for longer than most of its rivals, which gives an idea of how happy its learners are.

2.3 Artificial Intelligence MicroMasters

What is Artificial Intelligence MicroMasters? Artificial Intelligence MicroMasters is an AI 'mini-degree' offered by Colombia University, which you carry out through the edX web portal. You have 2 years to complete, and the university estimates it will take you at least 1.

Is Artificial Intelligence MicroMasters for experts or beginners? Counting as 25% of the Colombia Master's degree in Computer Science, should you wish to go that way, **Artificial Intelligence MicroMasters** by implication assumes at least an undergraduate knowledge of the subject.

Is Artificial Intelligence MicroMasters expensive? You can try it out for free, but the full **Artificial Intelligence MicroMasters** with credential will set you back £686 sterling – at the exchange rate at time of publishing – which is not exactly pocket change.

What are the benefits of Artificial Intelligence MicroMasters? **Artificial Intelligence MicroMasters** boasts worldwide recognition, including firms like GE, IBM, Volvo, Ford, Adobe and PwC. **Artificial Intelligence MicroMasters** will give you a good grounding in the nuts and bolts of AI. **Artificial Intelligence MicroMasters** gives learners a chance to apply the theory to practical real-world areas such as robotics, vision and physical simulation. **Artificial Intelligence MicroMasters** teaches neural network design. **Artificial Intelligence MicroMasters** offers a Machine Learning option.

What is Artificial Intelligence MicroMasters not so good at? **Artificial Intelligence MicroMasters** is not so good on brevity. They're offering some pretty comprehensive knowledge, but this is at least a year out of your life.

How popular is Artificial Intelligence MicroMasters? **Artificial Intelligence MicroMasters** has the approval of some of the big fish in industry, and Colombia has a certain cachet.

2.4 Google's ML Crash Course

What is Google's Machine Learning Crash Course? Google's Machine Learning Crash Course is part of the Google push to make AI available to all – a 15-hour introduction to machine learning.

Is Google's Machine Learning Crash Course for experts or beginners? Though you should be pretty familiar with maths (stats, algebra and maybe some calculus) and computers, **Google's Machine Learning Crash Course** is otherwise a course you could walk straight into off the street.

Is Google's Machine Learning Crash Course expensive? Google's Machine Learning Crash Course is completely free, and part of Google's plan to roll out their software to the general public.

What are the benefits of Google's Machine Learning Crash Course? Google's Machine Learning Crash Course will get you familiar with TensorFlow, the free Google AI library. **Google's Machine Learning Crash Course** uses case studies from the real world. **Google's Machine Learning Crash Course** offer video lectures from Google researchers. **Google's Machine Learning Crash Course** is just one of an increasing number of free courses being offered by Google.

What is Google's Machine Learning Crash Course not so good at?
Google's Machine Learning Crash Course is Google, and teaches through TensorFlow, which is also Google. So although it's free... it's all Google, and that may be a problem for some.

How popular is Google's Machine Learning Crash Course? Google's Machine Learning Crash Course has been taken by over 18000 Google engineers, and they can't ALL be wrong!

2.5 IBM Open Badge Programme

What is IBM Open Badge Programme? IBM Open Badge Programme on the IBM Skills Gateway offers learners a business understanding of AI processes and machine learning.

Is IBM Open Badge Programme for experts or beginners? While there are some beginner courses on offer, **IBM Open Badge Programme** is for those with a computer science educational background – medium to well-done, in steak terms.

Is IBM Open Badge Programme expensive? IBM Open Badge Programme may not be expensive, but they're teaching to use a platform that most certainly is, so – buyer beware.

What are the benefits of IBM Open Badge Programme? IBM Open Badge Programme boasts worldwide recognition and respect. **IBM Open Badge**

Programme focuses on the commercial applications of AI, including chatbots, image recognition and discovery services. **IBM Open Badge Programme** offers 3 "badges" of achievement: Explorer, Instructor and Author.

What is IBM Open Badge Programme not so good at? IBM Open Badge Programme is going to teach you how to use IBM Watson and IBM Cloud, and at some stage may ask you to move into an IBM house with an IBM spouse.

How popular is IBM Open Badge Programme? For people who love life in the IBM family, **IBM Open Badge Programme** is probably the way to go.

2.6 MIT's Deep Learning for Cars

What is MIT's Deep Learning for Self Driving Cars? MIT's Deep Learning for Self Driving Cars is a free lecture that tries to introduce the concept of AI through the reality of the self-driving car in 90 minutes.

Is MIT's Deep Learning for Self Driving Cars for experts or beginners? MIT's Deep Learning for Self Driving Cars is very accessible to the beginner, with nothing in the way of complex maths or coding.

Is MIT's Deep Learning for Self Driving Cars expensive? MIT's Deep Learning for Self Driving Cars is available online completely free of charge, as long as you don't turn up on MIT's doorstep asking for a degree anytime later.

What are the benefits of MIT's Deep Learning for Self Driving Cars? MIT's Deep Learning for Self Driving Cars is a nice way to get your head around the concept of AI. **MIT's Deep Learning for Self Driving Cars** uses a real-world example we are mostly familiar with – the car and driving – to show us what AI can and can't do. **MIT's Deep Learning for Self Driving Cars** is a video lecture with plenty of visual back-up.

What is MIT's Deep Learning for Self Driving Cars not so good at? MIT's Deep Learning for Self Driving Cars is not there to teach you how to actually *do* anything with AI, but then it doesn't claim to be.

How popular is MIT's Deep Learning for Self Driving Cars? MIT's Deep Learning for Self Driving Cars had nearly 44,288 views at time of writing.

2.7 NVIDIA Deep Learning Specialization

What is NVIDIA Deep Learning Specialization? NVIDIA Deep Learning Specialization promises its qualification will allow you to break into AI. The course is estimated (self-estimated, to be fair) to take 3 months at a pace of 11 hours a week, but you can of course go faster or slower if you want. All learning takes place online on the Coursera platform.

Is NVIDIA Deep Learning Specialization for experts or beginners? NVIDIA Deep Learning Specialization is not for experts (it says it will make you an expert, in fact) but it warns off beginners quite sternly.

Is NVIDIA Deep Learning Specialization expensive? NVIDIA Deep Learning Specialization is hard to pin down in terms of cost, but their 2-hour courses go for around $30, so we leave you to do the maths.

What are the benefits of NVIDIA Deep Learning Specialization? NVIDIA Deep Learning Specialization teaches learners to build models with a practical focus, so they are industry-ready by the end. **NVIDIA Deep Learning Specialization** introduces learners to Convolutional networks, RNNs, LSTM, Adam, Dropout, BatchNorm and Xavier/He initialization. **NVIDIA Deep Learning Specialization** teaches necessary elements of Python and TensorFlow. **NVIDIA Deep Learning Specialization** promises the graduate will be able to set up neural networks and act as a team leader on machine learning projects.

What is NVIDIA Deep Learning Specialization not so good at? NVIDIA Deep Learning Specialization is quite a commitment for the working man or woman, and is really aimed at those wanting to be quants one day.

How popular is NVIDIA Deep Learning Specialization? As with other components on the platform, **NVIDIA Deep Learning Specialization** gets a fair number of sign-ups.

2.8 Stanford University Machine Learning

What is Stanford University Machine Learning? Stanford University Machine Learning is an 11-week online course for learning about the basics of machine learning. Stanford University professor Andrew Ng (previously head of Baidu AI Group/Google Brain) is the creator and it uses the Coursera platform.

Is Stanford University Machine Learning for experts or beginners? With a very heavy workload (24 reading units just in Week 1), and a steep learning curve, it would be generous to say that **Stanford University Machine Learning** is for the techie with ambitions.

Is Stanford University Machine Learning expensive? Stanford University Machine Learning costs just £58, and is free if you don't want a certificate at the end or any marking. So that's very reasonable.

What are the benefits of Stanford University Machine Learning? Stanford University Machine Learning lets users grapple with backpropagation algorithms, error analysis and support vector machines. **Stanford University Machine Learning** introduces learners to MATLAB. **Stanford University Machine Learning** teaches through video lectures as well as text. **Stanford University Machine Learning** is flexible, so if you just can't meet a deadline, you can redo from that point at a later date.

What is Stanford University Machine Learning not so good at? Stanford University Machine Learning makes no concessions to time or depth, meaning you have to dive right in or not at all. Not for those who'd like to know how to use a few tools quickly and dirtily.

How popular is Stanford University Machine Learning? As you might imagine from the price vs content ratio, **Stanford University Machine Learning** is extremely popular.

2.9 Elements of AI

What is Elements of AI? Elements of AI is an online course from the University of Helsinki using the Independent platform. In 5-10 hours a week, for 6 weeks (though you can go at your own pace), the course promises to 'demystify AI'.

Is Elements of AI for experts or beginners? Elements of AI aims to be the course for beginners – with no difficult maths or coding skills required.

Is Elements of AI expensive? Elements of AI is absolutely free, compliments of Finland.

What are the benefits of Elements of AI? Elements of AI teaches what AI can do and – importantly – what it cannot. Elements of AI gets learners to grips with where AI will take us. Elements of AI explains how AI came about. Elements of AI enables you to critically evaluate the wild and outlandish claims made about AI every day.

What is Elements of AI not so good at? Elements of AI is very much a theoretical course, giving a nice grounding in the what of AI – but not the how. Lots of reading.

How popular is Elements of AI? On date of writing, 2600 students had at least dipped their toes in Elements of AI.

2.10 Fundamentals of Deep Learning for Computer Vision

What is Fundamentals of Deep Learning for Computer Vision? Fundamentals of Deep Learning for Computer Vision is an 8-hour course from Nvidia covering the AI subfield of teaching computers to see like us.

Is Fundamentals of Deep Learning for Computer Vision for experts or beginners? Though it's not an in-depth course in and of itself, since Fundamentals of Deep Learning for Computer Vision is a specialization within AI, it's a good idea to have some fundamentals of AI as a whole before tackling this.

Is Fundamentals of Deep Learning for Computer Vision expensive? Fundamentals of Deep Learning for Computer Vision is absolutely free, though you are of course tying your sleigh onto the Nvidia reindeer.

What are the benefits of Fundamentals of Deep Learning for Computer Vision? Fundamentals of Deep Learning for Computer Vision covers the technical basics of computer vision. Fundamentals of Deep Learning for Computer Vision will teach you to identify situations that would benefit from 'computer vision'. Fundamentals of Deep Learning for Computer Vision (as you might expect) leads you through the role Dr GPU (Nvidia) has played in making blind computers see.

What is Fundamentals of Deep Learning for Computer Vision not so good at? Fundamentals of Deep Learning for Computer Vision is a cool little intro to a specialization in the AI field, so it's really one of a number of airlocks leading out of the command module of AI, this one leading into the separate Vision module.

How popular is Fundamentals of Deep Learning for Computer Vision? A short snappy intro to a fast-expanding field + free of charge = very popular.

2.11 Learning from Data

What is Learning from Data? Learning from Data is a 10-week introductory course to machine learning on the Edx platform, asking the learner to put in between 10 and 20 hours per week.

Is Learning from Data for experts or beginners? Claiming to be aimed at absolute beginners, **Learning from Data** goes on to say that you're going to need some maths (including calculus), and knowing a programming language would 'help with homework'.

Is Learning from Data expensive? Learning from Data costs just $49 at time of writing – and that's if you want to be certified. Otherwise, it's free!

What are the benefits of Learning from Data? Learning from Data covers both theory and applications. **Learning from Data** teaches you to recognise algorithms. **Learning from Data** will help you master the maths and the use of heuristics in ML using real situations.

What is Learning from Data not so good at? Learning from Data is a fairly low-level course that requires some fairly high-level knowledge.

How popular is Learning from Data? Just because it's free, many programmers looking to shift over into AI and ML choose **Learning from Data.**

2.12 Grokking Deep Learning in Motion

What is Grokking Deep Learning in Motion? Grokking Deep Learning in Motion is a 5hr38m video course by Beau Carnes, which will introduce you to AI through 39 exercises.

Is Grokking Deep Learning in Motion for experts or beginners? While not aimed at absolute beginners, **Grokking Deep Learning in Motion** requires only a little programming knowledge (with Python specifically) and 'high-school math' (which sounds a little implausible).

Is Grokking Deep Learning in Motion expensive? Grokking Deep Learning in Motion is available for available $49.99, but there may be discounts available if you shop around.

What are the benefits of Grokking Deep Learning in Motion? Grokking Deep Learning in Motion is based on the very popular book of (nearly) the same name, *Grokking Deep Learning* by Andrew Trask. **Grokking Deep Learning** is presented by professional instructor Beau Carnes. **Grokking Deep Learning in Motion** doesn't attach you to any particular platform or library. **Grokking Deep Learning in Motion** boasts that by the end of the course you'll be able to build your own neural network – a bold claim indeed.

What is Grokking Deep Learning in Motion not so good at? Grokking Deep Learning in Motion is an ambitious attempt to put a popular book into a 21st century format. But can a 5hr38m video cover the material a 300page book does?

How popular is Grokking Deep Learning in Motion? Hard to tell, though the book certainly was.

2.13 CS188.1x: Artificial Intelligence

What is CS188.1x: Artificial Intelligence? CS188.1x: Artificial Intelligence is a 12-week online course from the University of Berkeley using the edX platform (though you choose your own pace). It will introduce you to the basics of AI – both theory and application.

Is CS188.1x: Artificial Intelligence for experts or beginners? CS188.1x: Artificial Intelligence is NOT for beginners – a probability of 1 that strong maths and coding skills are required.

Is CS188.1x: Artificial Intelligence expensive? CS188.1x: Artificial Intelligence is absolutely free of charge, though to get a certificate, you're going to have to spring.

What are the benefits of CS188.1x: Artificial Intelligence? CS188.1x: Artificial Intelligence will show you the applications of AI both now and in the future. CS188.1x: Artificial Intelligence involves practical work as well as theoretical – with a bias towards the former. CS188.1x: Artificial Intelligence will have you create your own agent capable of making guesses and predictions, as well as drawing conclusions. With CS188.1x: Artificial Intelligence, you will make your own algorithms for recognizing handwriting and photos.

What is CS188.1x: Artificial Intelligence not so good at? CS188.1x: Artificial Intelligence is pretty hard-core. Really only for the initiated, though the initiated do seem to love it.

How popular is CS188.1x: Artificial Intelligence? To date, 12900 students had investigated CS188.1x: Artificial Intelligence.

Appendix 3 - Blog: An Irreverent

Look At Data Science

Blog: An Irreverent Look At Data Science

<u>Regression & Logarithms By K Flynn:</u>
Should we regress to regression? The big data scientists' tool kit is full of incisive instruments but should he/she discard some of the blunter and more timeworn examples? Logistic Regression has pedigree and in my humble pie opinion should be retained as a wonderful classifying tool for use when the output is binary : x=0 or x= 1. In the context of consumer purchase the two values of x would be : x = buy or X = not buy A logistic algorithm would be built within the firm or a 'pretaplay' algo (off the shelf algos) can be purchased as long as the company IT team are competent and savvy. So either way using the example of the company 'Tasco's' we, the data team, would load in the data to train the algorithm. We would choose a logistic algo rather than a linear algo since we are interested in nonlinear relations. Even 'Little' can work out a straight line (unlike some of their inebriated customers). Put simply, a logarithm reduces large numbers to manageable integers as the human brain cannot fathom huge numbers as the majority of the populations deal in hundreds or thousands of ££. In our context the logarithmic algo allows us to produce the two values of x above. Once we have trained our algo, we move to purchase probabilities. Imagine Martin and 10 other 'Martins' are walking around Central London. Imagine it's Martin's wife's birthday and Martin is worried that his wife won't like her present. Last year he bought her chocolates and Diane, his wife, told him he was trying to get her fat. The year before that Martin bought Diane a pendant. Diane wore it on her birthday and when Martin asked about it six months later, Diane said she had lost it. (In reality, she hated the pendant and went back to the shop and took store credit). What will Martin buy? Since Martin and his wider family go to London shows we know their habits in terms of entertainment. We know their DOBs. Even though many people lie about the year of their birth online they usually tell the truth vis a vis month and day. We will have previous purchase information based on Diane's birthday, St Valentine's Day, Christmas and the many more days on which Martin is supposed to come up with a new present, always unique and imaginative. My sympathies are with Martin on this one. So sticking with x = buy or not buy with all of this information we would have a multi dimensional map in space through which with our logistic algorithm we can establish a 'relation', quantify according to our desired binary result and then send out ads to the Martins in London. So

as Martin thumbs his phone more and more desperately, wondering if he has time for a pint at O'Nialls, in real time an ad suggest he buy two tickets for the Spice Girls Reunion gig via the Tasco's website. Martin is aware of two things. One Diane loves the Spice Girls and two that Diane will want to go to the concert with her sister Helen, so Martin won't have to go. Bingo. Martin buys the tickets for delivery to his house. Job done. Within seconds Martin is in O'Nialls with two pints in front of him. He is smiling quietly to himself.

KNN By K Flynn:

Lazy Boy Algo brings home the bacon Just as in life where similar humans group together, so KNN or K Nearest Neighbour bunches together similar 'variables' which is the marketplace means 'consumers'. Despite being a simple algo, KNN has a massive advantage : it's the algo which travels light. All the computational part is left til last which is ideal for the GPS determined adverts sent to mobile phones to influence customer behaviour. Imagine we are looking at the late teen female market. On training data for last month's purchase data (2015 data is too old) we can use KNN to produce purchase types, price phenotypes, very much like the Spice Girls tried to cover the main categories of girls in the 90s (I won't bother rehashing their nicknames but now there maybe as many as 30 phenotypes with market value. Poor girls without money we will ignore because their 'demand' is not expressed in the marketplace). All of the females are voracious social media users in our sample, using it freely without the fear expressed by older consumers. Using real time calculations imagine these girls out shopping, often in packs, and we want to deliver buy selections to their mobiles. Say girl A (let's called her Alexandra) is sporty. This pattern is confirmed by her clothes sizes and types she buys and the low cal takeaways she eats. Say we know she is a member of a badminton club. The Olympics are approaching and, badminton being a major Olympic sport, we may predict that she (and 20 A girls like her) may buy a new outfit for her badminton games since she will know that more boys will be watching her games. Imagine she is near Lillywhite's in Piccadilly so an ad hits her phone with a selection of summer sporty outfits. We may also send an ad suggesting she visits the racket selection too. If we can get this A girl to share with her 4 girlfriends that's £40 x 4 = £160. Since we have 20 A girls like her that's £160 x 20 = £3.2K. These girls on a KNN would all map in space in the same cluster which measures distance between the girls of a particular market phenotype. We could do the same for 'scary spice' or 'goths' on their way to Camden market. Due to the recessive gene that produces ginger haired people, that market has probably declined too much to be relevant and as for that angry one well I wouldn't use KNN on her but perhaps

138

'Monte Carlo' or 'Brazilian'. In the past KNN has been used by the banks to predict loan defaults (and we saw where that got us with the subprimes). The grey suits with grey minds and grey souls. But KNN can also be happy smiley face too. Imagine if the 20 A girls turned up at my badders club I would get a tattoo with KNN on it! Super smiley, happy, vigorous girls. Super girls, Super Algo!

Centroids By K Flynn:
When Centroids lose their charm. The last two British elections have been called wrong by the political statisticians. The Tories were supposed to lose and even then we weren't supposed to have voted for Brexit. Why were these experts so wrong despite being right most of the time in the last 30 years? I will use one of the simpler big data algorithms to show why the pollsters tanked: K Means. Ironically K Means is probably one of the algos in the bag of tricks owned by our public opinion geniuses. But here's where they messed up. K Means is a clustering algorithm which requires the operator to fix the values a priori around which the variables will gather in clusters. These fixed values are called 'centroids' in the jargon and signify that based on previous results (elections in this case) the operator of the algo uses his/her expertise to guesstimate what will happen with new data (the election result). These centroid values are estimated mean values. So the big brains of MORI and their other chums made assumptions such as the Tories will lose as austerity had failed despite the elephant in the room being Labour's economists who plunged us into recession. Voters have memories that go back longer than 5 years! So when the experts inputted their set data to fix the centroids they omitted such facts. Again with Brexit wishful thinking overrode common sense the assumption that Cameron allied to the Labour Party with nothing specific on the table were a shoe in. These lazy assumptions again would have been used to program the machines wrongly. Back to K Means and assuming you have place your centroids judiciously, the learning data will spread out in space and associate with the nearest centroid based on the data values. Here comes the clever part: then the algorithm goes through multiple steps during which it centres itself on the mean point within the data clusters which are gathered around it. Finally the centroids stop moving and in the case of 2means cluster we get our answer ie Brexit yes or no. Intuitively we can see that the centroids move to the true centre of the respective cluster (assuming that the mean values of the data points is the 'true centre'). A valuable K Means analysis will minimize the distance between the n1 data points and the centroid value (k1) whilst at the same time maximizing distance from the second pole k2. This means the two groups are sufficiently separated beyond

possibilities for error (other than in extreme cases). Smiles all round ensue. So I guess then in conclusion that the maths majors running our polling industry will have to get out their screwdrivers and open the black box that keeps them in business. For the rules have changed and the algorithms need a boost. And given the incredible possibilities of the humble K Means algorithm we can conclude that 'he ain't heavy, he's my algo!'

SVM By K Flynn:

Support Vector Machines to out Sherlock Sherlock Imagine you are chasing down a dangerous criminal or 'forensic' as they are euphemistically monickered. The criminal world is protected by omerta if you talk you're dead and this coerced and brutal silence is enforced rigidly. 'Forensics' can be found in many places. Jail is an obvious one but on their false and feigned path to 'rehabilitation' they can be found in mental hospitals (the 'criminally' insane are in fact just crims in my experience) and hostels and homeless on the street. So we have set out the problem. Tradition policing involves networks of informers, bribery, infiltration of organized crime networks, setting one gang against another to flush out your prey (as in the Limerick gang on gang killings in 2015) and so on. Police men and women are notoriously careful. Despite the many movies they don't go wandering off by themselves into dangerous areas. What if traditional methods could be canned and the police could peacefully stick all the data into an SVM, send in the SWAT team and be home in time for tea? SVMs are amazing algorithms which work by classifying data into two categories : in this case dangerous criminals who are unrepentant (let's call them career criminals { CC }), RC (reformed criminals) and the whole mass of prisoners (let's designate them as TCP total criminal population. Below is a rough estimate of the criminal element in UK society. Total prison population in June 2016 was 85K so I have doubled that so that the number reflects those released. TCP = 85K x 2 = 170K CC ~= 10K RC ~= 160K We can train the SVM on old data. What SVM will do is categorize police records into two sets with a maximum distance between the two. Using two variables will produce a recognizable graph with an imaginary line separating the two sets of processed data. (a linear classifier). SVMs have another trick up their sleeve. They can handle extra variables so that the graph becomes 3 dimensional (three variables) or 4 dimensional (four variables) and so on which is increasingly difficult to visualize and understand for the layman or woman. However in the jargon there will be a 'plane' dividing the classified data. In our case CC instances would be separated from RC people.This is done using 'kernel' step. The police operator specifies a similarity function (a mathematical equation based on what you are looking for). This obviates the need to convert the whole data set into feature vectors which is laborious and time consuming for the machines. For example (a hunt to catch a master embezzler): S (j, r, d, sf, uf) = II j + r + d + sf + uf II to the power of 5 Where S = Suspect J = Job (+integer if person works in a bank) R = Responsible (+ integer if the person is a bank manager) D = Debt (+ integer if the person has major debts) Sf = (School friends + if some of them are criminals , negative if none are) UF = (same as for SF but concerning university friends) This type of embezzler (type a) then can be assigned a real number based on the equation above by the police operator and the S number triggers classification either as likely suspect or likely to be innocent (of this particular crime). Applied across the data set, names start dropping out of the hat and the gangs which have this specific modus operandi can be picked up and questioned. Not having been a policeman but as an avid fan of European noir detective fiction this above algorithm would be snapped up by police forces all over Europe to make their lives easier if that is not already the case. No excrement Sherlock!

Bayes By K Flynn:

The Bayesian Supremacy. The 20th Century was dominated by traditional statistics where a problem was studied and numbers generated to give results and models to act upon. This 'frequentist' modus operandi led to the huge blossoming of market research companies huge costly slow behemoths which are only now lumbering off the stage of history. The specialized companies like Mori mirrored their commercial cousins in plumbing public opinion and making predictions for party political performance in elections. But there are more ways to skin a cat (apologies to animal rights groups for the image). Bayesian algorithms had shown earlier promise 300 years ago but initially didn't make the grade. Now Bayes is the boy (and typically ignored by many university stats courses). The key distinction in Bayesian probabilities is the requirement for a priori distributions based on the premise that when we look at a new problem, our judgement is coloured by what we have learnt previously. In this way previous data (gathered in huge amounts by companies and governments alike) can be incorporated into the calculation. Decision makers often lack two factors when crunch point arrives: 1) Knowledge 2) Time. For example, we are two days away from the Brexit Referendum. Imagine you are a rich investor like George Soros who could predict the result with near certainty? Well then you would make a killing. Equally David Cameron's peace of mind would be considerable if he was sure of the outcome. Subjective Bayesian priors would be constructed using in the Brexit case: 1) Referendum results and election pathways in countries similar to Britain (ie Australia, Canada, New Zealand etc) 2) Recent opinion polls 3) Recent election results 4) Key events in election period (ie murder of Jo Cox) Then we proceed to the calculation of the Bayesian probabilities (posterior distribution) and happiness for David Cameron or funster Farage. Having said that, we are in the early stages of the utility of Bayes and his acolytes for humanity. Some Bayesian zealots are seeking 'objective' priors denuded of our human subjectivity with universal applications, something that would elevate Bayesianism to the Godlike status of Frigg the Norse deity. Thus decision makers (surrounded by their coteries of yes men and women telling them what they want to hear) would truly wield a blunderbuss. All rise for King Bayes!

Decision Trees By K Flynn:
The Mechanical Kraken Awakes. Of all the algorithms currently in use, decision trees are the most accessible to the comprehension of the lay man and woman. Those of you who programmed in BASIC in the 80s, or in my case C++ in the 90s, will recognize the formula : If $x = 0$ answer is negative If $x = 1$ answer is positive Where the value of x can mean a symptom for an illness such as pancreatic cancer. For example, if blood tests reveal that the enzyme amylase is not present in the patient or below threshold levels (amylase is used in the breakdown of carbohydrates) then this is an indicator of damage to the pancreas which is the gland that produces amylase. In this case $x = 1$. However, this may also be damage to the pancreas from another cause so the machine moves on to the next node which poses another question regarding a symptom of pancreatic cancer. If enough values $x = 1$ are reached, then the decision tree informs the operator that pancreatic cancer is suspected and further medical tests can be carried out. If $x = 0$ at the next node, then the algorithm pathway veers towards a result which says the patient is clear of the cancer though a subsequent $x = 1$ at the next node increases the likelihood of pancreatic cancer once again. In diagnosis, a medical problem is determined if say 6 out 10 symptoms are present. So that might mean 6 valuations of $x = 1$ and four of $x = 0$ and any combination of the symptoms (assuming no correlation between them). Thus the maze of the decision tree is created. In C++ the format is known generically as a flow control statement and the specific example here is known as 'branching'. They are called 'if statements' and so a decision tree is a vast array of 'ifs'. Oh those happy days of C++ when the world was simpler! Decision trees can be applied in a similar way to mental health diagnosis. Again out of an array of 10 symptoms only ~5 are needed to determine the illness. So in this scenario, the appearance of repeated suicidal ideation in the discourse of the

142

patient would result in x=1 and the technician could end up suspecting unipolar manic depression (where the patient's mental health problems are mainly of low mood to the extent of clinical depression). Then the specialist psychiatrist can be brought in to determine the treatment regime. A significant advantage to the use of this algorithm is that an expensive specialist is not needed to input the data, apply the decision tree algorithm and evaluate the results. In the era of stretched health budgets such savings are a boon. From the patient's point of view, though, there may be issues of data confidentiality since much personal medical data of theirs will be held on a machine and potentially could be lost or stolen. However, by imposing opt out on patients, this issue will be minimized. In conclusion however, the cost savings will out given the wide range of scenarios in which the decision tree algorithm can be used. And so the inexorable rise of the machines and their algorithmic runes will continue. Though we overpowered the organic Kraken, their mechanical descendants are quite another beast.

Random Forests By K Flynn:
Learning to see the forests and the trees In a country where mathematical knowledge is derided and ignorance on the topic celebrated in verse and song, persuading sales and marketing teams that your statistical analysis is relevant, can be an uphill battle. The simplest model relies on decision trees generating understandable rules which non maths staff can intuitively understand. For example, in terms of sales volume, a rule might be generated such that Price 20% = Sales + 5%. Everyone is happy and the sales team runs off and does what sales teams do. However decision trees have significant downsides such as 'overfitting'. This is when a model taught on a set of past data, models to the noise and not the essence. This tendency increases as the complexity of the data does. The worst case scenario is when the algorithm 'learns by heart' the training data especially if it's selection is based on performance with this data. (it is like when students memorize facts for exams without understanding the principles on which the facts are based). Of value however the company is predicting the future and increasing sales and this is how an algorithm should be evaluated and selected. Random Forests (RF) enhances the results on predictions and should be preferred. If for example Paddy Power is examining churn in its clients (losses of customers to Ladbrokes or 888 for example), the sales team want answers. Random Forests however aren't so intuitively understandable by nonmathematicians and the rules are not simplistic to comprehend which may cause 'resistance' within the company hierarchy. Also due to the complex processing needed for Random Forests a smaller subset of data is used in

143

training the algorithm. However the pearl amongst the swine of RF is that the algorithm can select the important parameters within the database, some of which may have been overlooked and use these insights to advise action by the sales team. These nodes generate branching into further decision trees.. It may be that Paddy Power has low loyalty for clients betting on premier league games due to the fact that their odds are less lucrative than the opposition. Once this is identified, the sales team can tempt clients with promotional odds (for example one off bets where money is refunded). Other decision trees generated by the RF algorithm can lead to further identification of anti churn actions and reactions. Your sales team may be resistant to you the data scientist's bag of tricks but your digital 'ecosystem' of forests and trees will slowly win them over, by which stage you will be the bear that found the honey.

Apriori By K Flynn:
Apriori to the rescue. Large supermarkets potentially cause headaches for those tasked with working out what products to put on the shelves and then choose the quantities to be stocked. Every inch of the shelves in the supermarkets is extremely valuable and fought over both by established brands and those trying to break into the market. Here is where algorithms can and do help by establish associations between different products. For example, if a big football match is coming up such as in the Euro 2016 tournament, then male customers will buy alcohol and snacks. Alcohol is used frequently in adverts given that cheaper alcohol will always attract buyers. Now men buy snacks with beer such as peanuts or crisps or even dried kangaroo meat. Apriori can analyse previous sales data to establish a relationship between how many beers are sold compared to snacks in a single purchase. Then the correct order can go out to the supermarket's warehouse to get the right proportions. Plus promotions can be put on to spur more purchases of snacks with beers. An alternative association might be strawberries and cream encouraged by Wimbledon. The operator decides which type of item set is being looked for ie 2item set, 3item set etc. The 'Support' is fixed by the operator and is the number of transactions containing the itemset divided by the total number of transaction. If this value is high, then it defines a frequent itemset. Confidence here is a % value defining the probability of customers buying beer and also buying a snack (given that some men will just buy beer or some will buy strawberries and pass on the cream). The Apriori algorithm first scans the database to quantify the 1 itemsets. Those that satisfy the support and confidence quantifiers go on to round 2, where 2 itemsets are defined. Round 3 would occur if a 3item set

was desired. Given that when Apriori is used with large data sets, it can be time consuming, then commercial examples of Apriori (ARTool, Weka and Orange are some examples) should be tested for efficiency in terms of time and accuracy. In 24 hour supermarkets this is indeed challenging!

BONUS BOOK: How to Manage Data Privacy & Compliance, Plus Improve Digital Channels in an AI World

Maurice 'Big Mo' Flynn FCIM FRSA FIDM MEng

Cantab

About the Author

Maurice 'BigMo' Flynn FCIM CMPRCA MEng Cantab

Maurice has **delivered learning events on these and related topics** for many of the biggest training companies in the UK, including the **CIM, ISMM, E-consultancy, DMA/IDM, DMI, British Council, IAB** and more. Over 30 years Maurice has trained thousands of people at hundreds of companies, including **Oracle, BBC, P&G and Google**. He is married to his business

 partner Antoaneta and they have two young boys. Feel free to contact 'Big Mo' via LinkedIn.

Testimonials

"Our members took a lot out of your logical GDPR approach." **Hotel Booking Agents Association (HBAA)**

"Supported Email Council hubs for 2+ years." **DMA**

"Top GDPR speaker & council member." **PRCA**

"Maurice has trained 100's of our clients." **CPA (CIM)**

"Helps you understand what is relevant to your situation. I can't recommend highly enough." **WeAreGecko.co.uk**

"Fantastic grounding in (GDPR) data protection." **YGAM**

"Excellent, well structured & informative." **FinsSwimClub**

"Quality info in easy to read & digestible format." **EkuaB.**

"Most clarity I've received from anywhere." **Armitt.co.uk**

"Cuts through the jargon and red tape, giving a practical focus on the steps to take." **Lenleys.co.uk**

"Our go to GDPR expert." **BreatheAgency.com**

"Helped with re-permissioning & privacy policy." **SunnyD**

"Intelligent approach to GDPR." **TMWUnlimited.com**

"Helping us complete our GDPR journey." **xxxx.com**

"Maurice is leading our GDPR prep." **iCrossing.com**

"Highly informative." **GBHealthcare**

All 5 ☆☆☆☆☆ Reviews on Amazon and Google!

Dedications and more …

These are the **collective opinions of Maurice 'Big Mo' Flynn** based on 30 years of relevant working experience and a **lifetime of learning and working with like minded experts**. They are therefore **not meant to be 100% perfect for everyone** - they are **simply meant to be generally useful!** They are especially relevant for **companies with limited resources** who are looking for a common sense approach.

Disclaimer: I'm not a lawyer so cannot dispense legal advice!

Dedicated to my mother, sister and brothers who never stop moving forward. Plus my wife and sons who get me out of bed in the morning, whether I want to or not. :)

Part 1-Data Compliance Post GDPR

Guess What?

Be warned ... **I'm not a lawyer** so won't be giving legal advice! This information is in fact curated from the **still evolving advice of the top experts** e.g. the ICO (Information Commissioner's Office), allied with my own hands on experience. Overall I wanted to develop an approach that is "**as simple as possible**" and helps delivers "**to do checklists**" applicable for all. Do let me know if I succeeded?

But First ... [Video Link]

What have you heard about GDPR? There is a lot of confusion, partly because some of the rules will **ultimately be clarified in the law courts**. But we can't wait around for that! We aim here to **focus on the essential business needs** as far as possible. P.S. In my content and events I like to **keep things interactive** and stimulating i.e. watch the videos, answer the questions and if possible share your own questions and opinions!

Expert Recommendations:

As you will see here I break the information into 4 sections throughout i.e. **general introductory information, important GDPR information, expert summaries and recommendations and detailed forms** which when completed, will help us build our GDPR prep plan and documentation. Here for example:

- Key principles for our preparation are **1. Data Privacy Management Ownership:** i.e. these relevant activities are embedded throughout the organisation; **2. Take Responsibility:** i.e. key activities are implemented and maintained by us; **3. Evidence:** i.e. this activity produces documentary evidence that shows our accountability and compliance.
- **Companies have been worried by the threat of EU fines of up to €20 million or 4% of total worldwide annual turnover** of the preceding

financial year, but the ICO has been clear that these compliance efforts will mitigate any penalties (GDPR Article 83). There is also the risk of **liability to 'data subjects'** if data leaks lead to financial or reputational damage and that situation would be resolved in a court of law and normally would depend on a combination of demonstrable compliance efforts and documented proof of damages (GDPR Article 82).

- **Existing related law**: We have plenty of laws that we currently follow and the majority of those continue of course, so we just need to adjust our approaches to take GDPR into account e.g. Employment contracts (GDPR Article 88), National ID's (GDPR Article 87), Freedom of expression (GDPR Article 85).

OK … are you still with me? Good - then let's get going on the first of the twelve steps for GDPR preparation!

Step 1: Raise awareness

What about?

We need to raise awareness of GDPR amongst our **senior management** - in the context of your own business model - as they are key to making change happen. We then need to raise awareness - in an organised and documented way - amongst our **employees and close partners, who come into contact with personal data**. Finally we need to raise **general awareness of the need for better personal data privacy practices for all our people,** to minimise the risks of human error, as well as document our commitment and compliance.

Start with the basics …
[Video Link]

The General Data Protection Regulation (GDPR) is a **regulation (i.e. legal)** by which the EU governing bodies will **strengthen and** unify personal data protection. It became applicable from **25th May 2018** and involves all people resident in **the EU* and their personal data**. Therefore it's relevant to **all companies dealing with the EU** (directly or via partners) and **all employees** - this includes **data controllers (gather data), processors (use data) and Data Protection Officers**. **Even post Brexit** the UK government plans alignment with GDPR.

* **EU**: Austria, Belgium, Bulgaria, Croatia, Republic of Cyprus, Czech Republic, Denmark, Estonia, Finland, France, Germany, Greece, Hungary, Ireland, Italy, Latvia, Lithuania, Luxembourg, Malta, Netherlands, Poland, Portugal, Romania, Slovakia, Slovenia, Spain, Sweden and the UK. **EEA**: Iceland, Liechtenstein and Norway.

Expert Recommendations:

In general and across all industries, GDPR experts are recommending **intensive training events for DPO's** and their companies, **tailored training events** for personal data handlers and general staff plus **online refreshers** for ongoing training and compliance documentation. **Independent auditing of compliance and internal tracking** of key compliance performance metrics as well as **documentary evidencing** is also recommended. **Documentation and prioritisation of risks are key elements!**

GDPR TRAINING AND AUDIT CHECKLIST

Subject	Last Completed	Next Date Planned (Quarterly)
DPO Training	NA	NA [Note: We are/not under 250 staff and use very small amounts of non sensitive data.]
Senior Management	Date:	Date:
Personal Data Handlers	Date:	Date:
All Staff and Partners	Date:	Date:
Board GDPR Performance Review	Date:	Date:
GDPR Compliance Audit	Date:	Date:

Document Control Reference: GDPR - Issue No: v1.1 - Issue Date: xx/xx/2018.

Signature1: _____ - Name - GDPR Project Leader

Signature 2: _____ - Name - Managing Director

Step 2: Complete data and risk audit

How?

Simply put, this means we need to **document all the personal data** we have and use, anywhere in our business or partner businesses. This personal data will be stored in a variety of places, including **official data storage facilities and informal places** e.g. on personal computers and mobile devices. It also means **non digital data** e.g. old reports and other documents. Just to reiterate we also need to include personal data that comes from or is shared **with business partners**. We need to **assess the GDPR compliance risks involved and plan to minimise.**

What's personal? [Video Link (00:53)]

Personal data is any data that can be used to **identify an individual person**. However it **doesn't just mean obvious stuff** like email addresses and mobile phone numbers. It includes **any** data that could be used to identify someone **eg IP address and even pseudonyms.** For all personal data we need to record **what permission was given** for that data and **when it expires.** We also need to know **how the data can be found, shared, amended and deleted**.

Expert Recommendations:

There is an **ongoing debate amongst experts** as to what extent **business contact information (B2B)** will be covered by GDPR. For now it's **safest to assume the worst** and plan for that, so that any "lightening" of the restrictions will be **a business upside!** (This is addressed in GDPR Article 5,6,30 and 39).

DATA AUDIT, FLOWS, RISK ASSESSMENT & GAP ANALYSIS

		Customers	Prospects	Employee
Personal Data	1.Email 2.name 3.address 4.mobile phone 5.landline 6.IP address 7. pseudonym 8. bank account 9. other?			
Where From	1.Data subject 2.partner 3.other 3rd party 4.government 5.other			
Legal Basis	1.Consent 2.contract 3.legal 4.legitimate interest 5.other			
How Used	1.Communication 2.credit scoring 3.other profiling 4.payment 5.other			
Who Uses	1.Marketing 2.sales 3.finance 4.IT 5. HR 6. other			
Where Stored	1.Local server 2.cloud server 3.desktop/laptop 4.hardcopy			

	5.other			
Who Shares?	1.Commercial partner 2.local government 3.national government 4.other			
Risks	1.Firewall hack 2.human error 3.lost device/data 4.internal hack 5.robbery 6.other			
Likelihood:	1.High 2.Medium 3.Low			
Impact:	1.High 2.Medium 3.Low			
Solution & Delivery Deadline	1.Update software patches - ongoing. 2. Data privacy & protection training - 6/3/2018 & 20/3/2018. 3. GDPR key processes - xxxx			

Document Control Reference: GDPR - Issue No:. 1.1 - Issue Date:.xxxx.

Signature1: _____ - xxxx - GDPR Project Leader

Signature 2: _____ - xxxx - MD

Step 3: Privacy policies

How?

There are new rules regarding **privacy notices, policies, rights and processes** that we all need to take into account. Businesses **need to first understand** these new requirements. Existing privacy notices need to be **amended (e.g. on your website) or new ones written in**

their absence. All **employees and data sharing partners will need training** about the new rights and processes, to avoid risk of human error.

The changes ... [Video Links 1 2]

Privacy policies and notices need to cover the **lawful basis** for collecting and processing personal data, plus **retention periods.** We also need to include the rights of the individual to **complain to the ICO, the right to be informed, to object, to access and rectify or erase, to restrict processing and automated decision-making** (eg profiling) plus **data portability** must all be simply explained

Experts Recommendations:

Some of the **largest companies have been preparing for GDPR** for years so keep an eye out for how your favourite big brands (eg Google, Microsoft, supermarkets et al) are adjusting their policies as this way **you can get free learning, courtesy of their 'reams' of legal resource!**

(This is addressed in GDPR Article 5,6,12-21,26,28 and 29).

DATA PRIVACY NOTICE CHECKLIST

	Privacy Policy Translate Website	Mobile Friendly & Timely	Phone & Verbal	Social Media Guide lines
Explains What Personal Data Is Used & How & Why It's Used	Y/N	Y/N	Y/N	Y/N
Explains How Long It's Used For & How It's Kept Secure	Y/N	Y/N	Y/N	Y/N
Explains Who Uses the Data ie Internal & External	Y/N	Y/N	Y/N	Y/N

Explains the Legal Basis for Data Usage	Y/N	Y/N	Y/N	Y/N
Explains Your Rights eg Portability, Erase, Amend and Restrict Plus Contact Info	Y/N	Y/N	Y/N	Y/N
Easy To Find, Understand & Accessible	Y/N	Y/N	Y/N	Y/N

Document Control Reference: GDPR - Issue No:. 1.1 - Issue Date:.xxxx.

Signature1: _____ - xxxx - GDPR Project Leader

Signature 2: _____ - xxxx - MD

Step 4: Prepare data requests

How?

Companies using personal data need to be ready to **respond at short notice** to data requests from the individual. Most companies **do not have the resources** or tools to do this reliably and **failure penalties are potentially high**. We need to first understand these new requirements and put in place the **people, processes and tools** to ensure compliance. All **employees and data sharing partners will need training** about the new processes to avoid risk of human error.

The requests ...
[Video Link]

Data requests from individuals can relate to any of the **rights mentioned in step 3 i.e. rights to object, be informed, access, rectify,** erase, restrict processing and automated decision-making plus portability. Companies have **one month (30 days) to respond** and **cannot charge** for these data requests, unless excessive. **If a company refuses**, it must **communicate why as well as the right to complain** for independent judgement eg via the ICO.

Expert Recommendations:

Responding to data requests is essential but few companies have the processes in place to comply reliably. **It's also hard to anticipate how many we might receive.** Smaller companies are tending to **set up manual processes** until the size of demand is clearer. Larger companies look to use **semi automated software tools** as probably the best scalable solution to use, especially when we're trying to **find all the data in multiple places**.

(This is addressed in GDPR Article 6,12,15-22).

SUBJECT ACCESS RECORD (SAR) REQUEST PROCESS

	Data Subject or Legal Request
Policy	At xxxx we acknowledge that protecting the privacy of people's personal data is important. We recognise that people have rights with regards their personal data ie to be informed, to access, to rectify, to erase, to opt out of profiling and automated decision making and to port that data elsewhere. We are committed to ensuring people's personal data is managed competently by:: Ensuring compliance with all relevant legislation as a minimum. Setting and reviewing performance against objectives and targets that drive continuous improvements in our compliance in this area. Providing sufficient information, resources and training to facilitate the achievement of our objectives in this area. Overall responsibility for data privacy and protection in line with GDPR rests with the Executive Board. The Executive Board discharges this responsibility through the Divisions teams who are responsible for the implementation of this Policy. This Policy statement applies to the whole xxxx company and is available to all employees via our intranet. The policy is also made publicly available on our website. The contents of this Policy will be reviewed and updated as necessary on at least an annual basis.
Process	**Week 1: Authenticate & clarify request - xxxx GDPR Project Lead** **Week 2: Complete internal processes: - xxxx GDPR Project Lead** - **Inform:** List of data we have, what we use if for & how long, who we share it with. - **Object/Rectify/Erase/Access/Port:** Where is the data stored? - **Opt out of profiling:** Where do we record opt outs? **Week 3: Complete processes: - xxxx GDPR Project Lead**

Templates	Dear Sir/Madam,
	Thank you for your recent message, requesting"xyz.
	"Please could you confirm the following in writing:
	- That you are NAME and provide documentary evidence eg passport photocopy.
	- That you want us to do the following:
	    - Inform you of the personal data we have for you, what we use if for & how long and who if anyone we share it with.
	    - Rectify your personal data as follows "xyz."
	    - Erase your personal data from our systems.
	    - Send you your personal data in a convenient file format eg hard copy or pdf or CSV file? Where is the data stored?
	    - Opt you out of personal profiling and/or automated decision making.
	
	We aim to complete this within 30 days as required and will keep you informed.
	
	Kind regards etc.
	
	---------- 	
	
	Dear Sir/Madam,
	Thank you for your recent message, requesting"xyz.
	We are pleased to confirm completion of this task as requested ie
	    - Inform you of the personal data we have for you, what we use if for & how long and who if anyone we share it with.
	    - Rectify your personal data as follows "xyz."
	    - Erase your personal data from our systems.
	    - Send you your personal data in a convenient file format eg hardcopy or pdf or CSV file? Where is the data stored?
	    - Opt you out of personal profiling and/or automated decision making.
	
	Kind regards etc.

Accessible	Yes
Tracking	Yes

Multichannel	Yes
Automated	NA
	Eg 1.Preference Centre 2.Customer Login 3. Customer Service Mailbox 4.Other

Document Control Reference: GDPR - Issue No:. 1.1 - Issue Date:.xxxx

Signature1: _____ - xxxx - GDPR Project Leader

Signature 2: _____ - xxxx - MD

Step 5: Lawful basis for data

How?

Companies holding and using personal data need to be **clear on the lawful basis** for doing so and **document** that for evidencing on request. Companies can **no longer keep records of personal data indefinitely** or without detailed documentation as to why. **Individuals, supervisory bodies (the ICO) and courts** all can request access to that information at short notice. We need to first understand **what is permitted** under GDPR and put in place the **people, processes and tools** to ensure compliance. All **employees and data sharing partners will need training** about the new processes to avoid risk of human error.

It's the law dude ...
[Video Links 1 2 9:00]

Companies are permitted to hold and use personal data under any one of the following provisos. If **Consent** is given from the individual concerned; by **Contract** ie legal agreement; by **Law** if required eg employment law; if **Vital** eg for life-or-death scenarios; if for **Public** task eg courts; if **Legitimate Interests**, where we must **balance the legitimate interests and rights of all parties** e.g. the individual's **right to privacy** and businesses' **commercial need to communicate and find new solutions** to business challenges.

Expert Recommendations:

Many companies have personal data captured over the years but with little or poor quality **documented consent.** Many companies have generalised databases where lot's of different **sources of data intermingle**. This all need to be untangled and **cleaned up fast**!

(This is addressed in GDPR Article 5,6).

LAWFUL BASIS RECORD

	Consent 1.Evidence? 2.Duration?	Contract?	Legitimate Interest?
Customer Data	?	?	?
Prospect Data	?	?	?
Employee Data	?	?	?
Other Data	?	?	?

Document Control Reference: GDPR - Issue No:. 1.1 - Issue Date:.xxxx

Signature1: _____ - xxxx - GDPR Project Leader

Signature 2: _____ - xxxx - MD

Step 6: Correct consent & legitimate use

How?

Many businesses use personal data which has been captured over months or years but with **poor quality consent documentation or legitimate use justification.** Many businesses have centralised databases where lots of different **sources of data intermingle**. All personal data that has not been correctly consented to must be re-assessed. We need to understand **what consent and legitimate use means under GDPR and audit our data accordingly**. Compliant data can be used for the **permitted time period. Non compliant data must be deleted or re-permissioned.**

Was that a yes?
[Video Link 1]

Under GDPR consent must be **freely given, specific, informed and unambiguous.** It requires a positive opt-in i.e. it **cannot be inferred** via pre ticked boxes and must be definitive. Consent agreements must be **separate from other T&C's** i.e. not hidden. It also must be **simple to withdraw** consent at any time. Legitimate use means we must **balance the legitimate interests and rights of all parties** e.g. the individual's **right to privacy** and businesses' **commercial need to communicate and find new solutions** to business challenges.

Expert Recommendations:

Many companies have personal data captured over the years with little or poor quality **documented consent and legitimate use justification.** Many companies have generalised databases where lots of different **sources of data intermingle**. This all need to be untangled and **cleaned up fast**!

(This is addressed in GDPR Article 5,6 and 12).

DOCUMENTING CONSENT & LEGITIMATE INTEREST

	Consent & Expiry	How Authenticate?	Legitimate Interest?
Prospect Data			
Partner Data			
Other Data			

Document Control Reference: GDPR - Issue No:. 1.1 - Issue Date:.xxxx

Signature1: _____ - xxxx - GDPR Project Leader

Signature 2: _____ - xxxx - MD

Step 7: Rules for kids & sensitive data

How?

As you might expect **childrens' and other sensitive data merits extra protection** although it **can vary by country**. The main issue for kids is **from whom the consent permission** came and **are they old enough** to be legally responsible? For sensitive data (e.g. race or ethnic origin, politics, religion, trade union status, health, sex preference, criminal record) we can **only use it in restricted ways**. Sensitive data has also been extended to include genetic data and biometric data. We need to understand **what consent for children means under GDPR and audit our data accordingly**. We also need to be clear on **how other sensitive data can be used**. Compliant data can be used for the **permitted time period. Non compliant data must be deleted or re-checked eg for permission or another lawful basis.**

How old are you?

In the UK it is proposed that under GDPR children can give their own consent to personal data usage **at 13 years and above although this has still not completed Parliamentary approval**. Other countries will set the age limit **between 13-16 years** and are also finalising their plans. Under these age limits consent must be obtained from the **parent or legal guardian**. Sensitive data use (eg health, ethnicity, criminal records et al) **must comply with all existing restrictions (e.g. minimised use for lawful tasks) with added transparency under GDPR. Public bodies cannot rely on "legitimate interest." Criminal record data usage is further restricted.**

Expert Recommendations:

One of the key challenges here is the **different treatment of children by age of consent across countries**. For sensitive data **specialist advice is recommended if this is a big part of the business model.** (This is addressed in GDPR Article 8,9 and 10).

Step 8: Data breach response

How?

Until now companies have often **kept quiet about data breaches, hacks and leaks** as there was little incentive to go public but that's all changing. We now need to **report personal data breaches very quickly or risk big fines**. Most companies recognise they don't currently have the people, processes or tools to do this scalably. We need to first understand **what is required** under

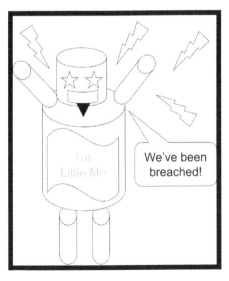

GDPR and put in place the **people, processes and tools** to ensure compliance. All **employees and data sharing partners will need training** about the new processes to avoid risk of human error.

What to do? [Video Link]

Personal data breaches must be reported to the Information Commissioner's Office (ico.org.uk) **within 72 hours** or we risk fines of up to 20m Euros or 4% global turnover, whichever is larger! Data breaches must also be reported to the individuals involved without delay if "high risk" ie **if likely to risk the rights of individuals eg via discrimination, reputation, financial loss, loss of confidentiality or any other significant economic or social disadvantage.**

Expert Recommendations:

Imagine trying to deal manually with a data breach at **midnight on 25th December** or other big national holidays! Smaller companies are tending to **set up manual processes** to prepare cost effectively. Larger companies are looking to use **semi automated software tools** as probably the best scalable solution.

(This is addressed in GDPR Article 12 and 33).

DATA BREACH RECORD CHECKLIST

Policy	At xxxx we acknowledge that protecting the privacy of people's personal data is important. We recognise that people have rights with regards their personal data ie to be informed, to access, to rectify, to erase, to opt out of profiling and automated decision making and to port that data elsewhere. We are committed to ensuring people's personal data is managed competently by:: Ensuring compliance with all relevant legislation as a minimum. Setting and reviewing performance against objectives and targets that drive continuous improvements in our compliance in this area. Providing sufficient information, resources and training to facilitate the achievement of our objectives in this area. Overall responsibility for data privacy and protection in line with GDPR rests with the Executive Board. The Executive Board discharges this responsibility through the Divisions teams who are responsible for the implementation of this Policy. This Policy statement applies to the whole xxxx company and is available to all employees via our intranet. The policy is also made publicly available on our website. The contents of this Policy will be reviewed and updated as necessary on at least an annual basis.
72 Hour Process	<ul><li>**Day 1: Authenticate, confirm & fix breach - xxxx GDPR Project Lead**</li><li>**Day 2: Prepare documentation: - xxxx GDPR Project Lead**</li></ul> **Ie Inform ICO - Assess Risk & Inform Subject - Review & Future Proof** <ul><li>**Day 3: Complete process: - xxxx GDPR Project Lead**</li></ul>
Templates	Dear Sir/Madam, Thank you for your recent message, requesting"xyz. "Please could you confirm the following in writing: - That you are NAME and provide documentary evidence eg passport photocopy. - That you want us to do the following: - Inform you of the personal data we have for you, what we use if for & how long and who if anyone we share it with. - Rectify your personal data as follows "xyz." - Erase your personal data from our systems. - Send you your personal data in a convenient file format eg hardcopy or pdf or CSV file? Where is the data stored? - Opt you out of personal profiling and/or automated decision making.

	We aim to complete this within 30 days as required and will keep you informed. Kind regards etc. ---------- Dear Sir/Madam, Thank you for your recent message, requesting"xyz. We are pleased to confirm completion of this task as requested ie - Inform you of the personal data we have for you, what we use if for & how long and who if anyone we share it with. - Rectify your personal data as follows "xyz." - Erase your personal data from our systems. - Send you your personal data in a convenient file format eg hard copy or pdf or CSV file? Where is the data stored? - Opt you out of personal profiling and/or automated decision making. Kind regards etc.
Accessible - **Multichannel -** **Tracked -** **Automated**	- Yes - Yes - Yes - NA

Document Control Reference: GDPR - Issue No:. 1.1 - Issue Date:.xxxx

Signature1: _____ - xxxx - GDPR Project Leader

Signature 2: _____ - xxxx - MD

Step 9: Protection by design

How?

Many companies have as many data leakage risks as an old watering can has water leaks! **Employees roam the world accessing and sharing personal data on a variety of devices and systems** only some of which are secure. GDPR means this cannot continue. A better approach means **rethinking personal data usage** in your company and **ensuring it cannot leak by design** rather than by accident. Most companies recognise they don't currently have the people, processes or tools **to do this scalably**. We need to first understand **what is required** under GDPR and put in place the **people, processes and tools** to ensure compliance.

By design?
[Video Link]

Protection by design means building privacy into every process and system **from the ground up** and from scratch if needed. We can **map the flows of data** and **cut out areas of risk** eg human error. To get there we need to **minimise & delete, protect, anonymise, pseudonymise & encrypt, inform, give access & automate**.

Data Protection Impact Assessments are for new, high risk areas e.g. new projects and data transfers. **Within 8 weeks of submitting a DPIA** (plus an additional 6 weeks may be required for complex cases), the supervisory authority (i.e. in the UK this is the ICO) **will give advice on whether the intended project has GDPR issues.**

Expert Recommendations:

For big companies with large amounts of data <u>**this is a big set of changes and requirements - see example checklist overleaf**</u>. For smaller companies <u>**this is less onerous - see underlined elements overleaf.**</u>

(This is addressed in GDPR Article 5,24,25 and 32).

PRIVACY BY DESIGN CHECKLIST

Integrated with InfoSec Policy eg ISO270001	Y / N
Data classification procedure	Y / N
Encryption technology and processes	Y / N
Identity Access Management (need to know basis)	Y / N
Software tools for aggregation, data masking, pseudonymisation, and anonymisation	Y / N
Policy and procedure on pseudonymisation or anonymization	Y / N
	Y / N
Enterprise privacy risk assessment and mitigation plan	Y / N
	Y / N
Audits of methodology	Y / N
Record retention policy	Y / N
Application development protocols	Y / N
Project security risk assessments	Y / N

	Y / N
Security of processing	Y / N
Perimeter security measures	Y / N
System monitoring	Y / N
Acceptable use policy	Y / N
Information security audit of system access privileges	Y / N
Password parameters	Y / N
Data center security measures (e.g., biometrics, access restriction, monitoring)	Y / N
Electronic badge access system - Physical records room with locked doors	Y / N
Restricted access to backup tapes and media	Y / N
Clean desk policy	Y / N
Employee agreement outlines security responsibilities	Y / N
Employee termination checklist	Y / N

Employee background checks	Y / N
Data loss prevention (DLP) software	Y / N
Data privacy and security requirements for third parties	Y / N
	Y / N
Contracts with third parties processing data	Y / N
Business continuity plan	Y / N
Job descriptions for data protection-related roles	Y / N
Contract templates for DPO functions (if outsourcing)	Y / N
Defined privacy roles and responsibilities	Y / N
Privacy steering committee	Y / N
Data protection training and awareness materials	Y / N
Data protection as a regular agenda-item for the board	Y / N
	Y / N
Data protection impact assessment templates	
Data protection impact assessment guidelines	Y / N

Budget for the DPO function	Y / N
Policy on conflict of interests	Y / N
Formal reporting structures	Y / N
Procedures for handling inquiries and complaints	Y / N
Data privacy notice	Y / N
Procedures or guidance on when to seek DPO input	Y / N
Document Control Procedure GDPR	Y / N
Data Protection Policy Review Procedure GDPR	Y / N
Contact with Authorities Work Instruction	Y / N
Storage Removal Procedure	Y / N
Third Party Contracts	Y / N
External Parties – Information Security Procedure	Y / N
Reporting Information Security Weaknesses and Events Procedure	Y / N
Responding to Information Security Reports	Y / N

Collection of Evidence Procedure	Y / N
Control of Records Procedure	Y / N
Monitor and Measurement Register	Y / N
Audit Schedule	Y / N
Audit Lead Report Sheet	
Management Review Record	
Schedule of Authorities and Key Suppliers	
Removal of Information Assets	
Information Security Event Reports	

Document Control Reference: GDPR - Issue No:. 1.1 - Issue Date:.xxxx

Signature1: _____ - xxxx - GDPR Project Leader

Signature 2: _____ - xxxx - MD

DATA PROTECTION IMPACT ASSESSMENT

What is the aim and description of the project?	
What personal data will be collected?	
How will the personal data be collected?	
Where will the personal data be stored?	
Where will the personal data be shared?	
How will the personal data be amended or deleted?	
GDPR risks identified (individual, organisational, compliance)?	
Solutions identified (individual, organisational, compliance)?	
Other safeguards, security measures and mechanisms to ensure compliance?	

Document Control Reference: GDPR - Issue No:. 1.1 - Issue Date:.xxxx

Signature1: _____ - xxxx - GDPR Project Leader

Signature 2: _____ - xxxx - MD

Step 10: Data protection officer

Must We?

Bigger companies (250+ employees) using lots of personal data are **compelled to have a data protection officer**. Smaller companies are not be but the principles of the role help **avoid some of the risks** associated with

GDPR compliance **eg ownership/ responsibility**.

Companies need to assess the mandatories and risks and **look at in house vs outsourced requirements.**

Tell me officer?

[Video Links 1 0:07 2 0:14]

A DPO is mandatory for **public bodies, large users of sensitive data or if you undertake large scale, regular and systematic monitoring of data subjects.** Many larger companies also find it the best way to manage the GDPR risks and processes and **ensure ownership**. The DPO should be a data privacy law **expert;** advise the Controller or Processor and its employees of **data protection obligations**; monitor **compliance, including assigning responsibilities**, training and audits; advise on and monitor **DPIA impact assessments**, cooperate with and contact the **supervisory authority and data subjects** as required; be involved in **all issues** relating to processing personal data; ensure **sufficient resources**, act in an **independent** manner, with direct reporting to the **highest management level.** It is not a role to be allocated lightly.

Expert Recommendations:

For larger companies having a DPO **ensures ownership** of the responsibilities of GDPR compliance. **In house if resources allow but can be contracted if resources/expertise lacking.**

For smaller companies there may not be enough work for a full time DPO. **In this case a well resourced cross functional team, with a clearly identified team leader plus senior management sponsorship, should suffice.**

(This is addressed in GDPR Article 38 and 39).

Step 11: International preparation

Where?

The EU's governing bodies **want to deal with local contacts** when it comes to issues of GDPR compliance so companies will have to select and document who and where that is (called your **"lead data protection supervisory authority"**). Employees and partners should **also be made aware. Personal data transfers to countries outside the EU and a short list of approved countries** are also restricted.

Around the world? [Video Links 1 9:19 2]

Your lead data protection supervisory authority is your supervisory authority **in the state where your main establishment is.**

Your main establishment is your **EU central administration or the location where data decisions are made.** Personal data transfers between countries and outside the EU **must be made under certain secure, approved processes only - see overleaf.**

Expert Recommendation:

For UK companies your lead office will be **UK HQ until after Brexit.** For European companies this will be **European HQ** most of the time, unless local factors intervene. **Data transfer rules** are still under debate in some areas - see overleaf.

(This is addressed in GDPR Article 27 and 45-49).

INTERNATIONAL DATA
TRANSFER PROCESS

1. **Is the personal data transfer within EU?**	Y/N
2. **Is personal data transfer to country with "adequate data protection laws"? e.g. Canada, Switzerland (http://ec.europa.eu/justice/data-protection/international-transfers/adequacy/index_en.htm)**	Y/N
3. **Is personal data transfer with USA under EU-US Privacy Shield? (NB Ongoing issues.)**	Y/N
4. **Is personal data transfer using Binding corporate rules BCR's and/or legal contracts?**	Y/N

Document Control Reference: GDPR - Issue No:. 1.1 - Issue Date:.xxxx

Signature1: _____ - xxxx - GDPR Project Leader

Signature 2: _____ - xxxx - MD

Step 12: Plan of attack

How?

Big companies have been preparing for GDPR for years. Some **smaller companies** haven't started. It's not too late of course but we all need to **start now and focus on the priorities.**

Let's Prioritise!

The key elements for attacking GDPR prep with speed and accuracy are generally agreed to be the following:

1. A cross functional Data Privacy Steering Committee with a board level sponsor and expert external partners if needed;

2. Data audit, risks, gaps and data flow analysis;

3. Project timeline, resources and tools;

4. Data protection and privacy policy i.e. summary of all the previous sections, tailored for your business.

Expert Recommendations:

This does not have to be too difficult if you **start today & prioritise!**

PROJECT PLANNING

Prep Steps	Risk Level (Circle)	Resource Level (Circle)	Lead Times Estimate (Mths) (Circle)
1 Awareness	**High** / Medium / Low	High / Medium / **Low**	**1-2** / 3-4 / 5+
2 Audit	**High** / Medium / Low	**High** / Medium / Low	1-2 / **3-4** / 5+
3 Privacy Policy	**High** / Medium / Low	High / **Medium** / Low	1-2 / **3-4** / 5+
4 Requests	**High** / Medium / Low	High / **Medium** / Low	1-2 / **3-4** / 5+
5 Lawful Basis	**High** / Medium / Low	High / **Medium** / Low	1-2 / 3-4 / **5+**
6 Consent/Legit	**High** / Medium / Low	**High** / Medium / Low	1-2 / 3-4 / **5+**
7 Kids & Sensitive Data	High / **Medium** / Low	High / **Medium** / Low	1-2 / 3-4 / **5+**
8 Data Breach	**High** / Medium / Low	High / **Medium** / Low	1-2 / **3-4** / 5+
9 Privacy By Design / DPIA	High / **Medium** / Low	**High** / Medium / Low	1-2 / 3-4 / **5+**
10 DPO	High / **Medium** / Low	**High** / Medium / Low	1-2 / 3-4 / **5+**
11 International	High / **Medium** / Low	**High** / Medium / Low	1-2 / 3-4 / **5+**
12 Plan	**High** / Medium / Low	**High** / Medium / Low	1-2 / **3-4** / 5+

Document Control Reference: GDPR - Issue No:. 1.1 - Issue Date:.xxxx

Signature1: _____ - xxxx - GDPR Project Leader

Signature 2: _____ - xxxx - MD

Part 2 - Digital Channels Post GDPR

Whazzup?

Now that we're **up to speed with GDPR compliance**, let's take a look at our **digital channels and how we can optimise** those further. **Some of this is quite advanced** on the assumption most companies have been using these channels for years but in all cases there are **simple improvements outlined that we can all benefit from as well as intermediate and advanced steps**. We will **focus on areas of most relevance to all.**

How can we all improve?

[Video Link 1]

Expert

Recommendations:

Based on my work with 100's of companies, **most companies digital channels can be significantly improved in 4 areas which are: Reach, Cadence, Personalisation and Social Shares.** I'll explain these areas in the context of the different digital channels and the content we should use there.

2.1 Email CRM automation and databases

How?

There are several key ways to better engage customers and stakeholders: **Reach i.e % of target audience, Cadence i.e. timing, Personalisation and activating Social Sharing**. Most marketers **don't pull all these levers** to the max and don't automate enough for **scalability**. Over the years email has been seen as a **niche tool** and it's also been **too profitable** for its own good. **Confusion over permission** hasn't helped. As a marketing practice it needs to **grow up and take its rightful leading place** at the business table. Email is a **key identifier** for the digital age - this has pro's and con's of course. Companies need to ensure their strategy is mature and **integrated.**

Four areas of improvement:

Reach - How can I find more of my targets eg via email?

Cadence - How do I decide the optimum send frequency and time?

Personalisation - What's the right content and why?

Social - How can I motivate sharing?

Expert Recommendations:

- Big Mo's **eCRM Improvement Grid**: See below.

- **Example Video Links:** Apparel - Charity - Engineering - Media/Events - MicroSME - Retail/Ecommerce - Pharma/Healthcare - Telco - Legal - Travel - Property - ITC

Big Mo's eCRM Improvement Grid:

TARGET	1.Reach	2. Cadence	3.Personalise
NEED	Data Partners	Time of send analysis + control tools.	Personalisation analysis + control tools.
TOOLS	Data Partners: Experian / Creditsafe / Acxiom (use Test Samples)	Via Email Service Provider or use Excel + Extension Library (Predictive Analytics)	ESP Via Partner (App) Library (eg Altaire.com)
FINANCE ANALYSIS	Todays SimpleAI .com	Todays SimpleAI .com	Todays SimpleAI .com
EXAMPLE	Sport/Bet, All Retail, Travel, Finance, B2B, SME, Other	Sport/Bet, All Retail, Travel, Finance, B2B, SME, Other	Sport/Bet, All Retail, Travel, Finance, B2B, SME, Other

2.2 Content creation inc PR crisis comms

Latest Insights

We never have enough content right? **Yet we all create content all day long** when we speak to people, share opinions, write emails, post on Facebook and even show stuff with our hands and facial gestures. However when

it comes to content creation for digital channels **all too often we panic** and think it's too hard, time consuming or risky.

So What To Do?

My approach is to capture more of the day to day content that is created in every business and **use simple tools to spin that rough stuff into content gold**!

Expert Recommendations:

- Big Mo's **Content Improvement Grid**: See Below.

- **Example Video Links: Charity**

Big Mo's Content Improvement Grid:

CONTENT	1. Text / Images	2.Audio/Video /Animation	3.Crisis
NEED	Audio tran scription & auto generation - screen capture	Easy to use video/audio /animation tools	Replace ment content on dark sites
FREEMIUM TOOLS	Youtube MTurk Wordsmith Jing Giphy EnhanceNet	Animoto GHangout Youtube Enhance	Wordpress 1Wordpres s2 Pre crisis rehearse - Post crisis - see SEO
FINANCIAL ANALYSIS	Todays SimpleAI .com	Todays SimpleAI .com	Todays SimpleAI .com
EXAMPLES	Marketing agencies	Marketing agencies	British Council

2.3 Twitter, Facebook, LinkedIn & ads

Latest Insights

Social media seems to have **taken over the world** at times - from elections to legal debates to celebrity culture and everything in between. The dominant platforms have **become mainstream** - the newer platforms will **often be bought up** before they can compete or alternatively drowned out. Of course the younger generation will always seek the **new, lower cost channels**.

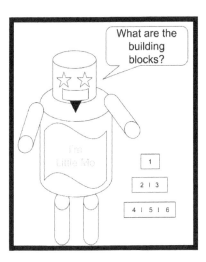

OK What Now?

Nowadays I look at social media as **simply more channels** for dialogue and engagement so the **questions to consider** become: are **your customers and stakeholders** there and if so what, if anything, **might they want from you there?** We need to download our data from social media platforms so we can **analyse it better and understand which content really works well i.e.drives commercial value and ROI**. Ads online allow you to boost your reach **once you know what the commercial value is.**

Expert Recommendation:

- Big Mo's **Social Improvement Grid**: See below.
- Example Video Links: Property1 2 3 4 5 6

Big Mo's Social Improvement Grid:

PLATFORM	Facebook Twitter	LinkedIn	Other	Ads
NEED	Analyse better what drives more positive engagement	Analyse better what drives more positive engagement	Analyse better what drives more positive engagement	Amplify success
TOOLS	Extract data via FacebookApps or SimplyMeasured & Trackur	Extract data via Hootsuite	Test and learn via Pinterest Snapchat Whatsapp	Facebook Ads GAdwords AmazonAds
FINANCIAL ANALYSIS	Todays SimpleAI .com	Todays SimpleAI .com	Todays SimpleAI .com	Todays SimpleAI .com
EXAMPLE	Sport/Bet, All Retail, Travel, Finance, B2B, SME, Other	Marketing Agencies	Marketing Agencies	Sport/Bet, All Retail, Travel, Finance, B2B, SME, Other

2.4 Websites, blogs, apps & SEO

Latest Insights

We'll focus again here on key drivers of customer and stakeholder growth and satisfaction: **reach, cadence,**  **personalisation and social shares**. To do this best we need to **solve people's problems and answer their questions**, in a quick and engaging style. **Websites** need to personalise more, **blogs** need to share more and **apps** are for loyalty if needed. SEO will change a lot with **audio, visual and even AI search** so let's get the **basics right first**.

Areas of improvement:

- **Reach** - How can I find more of my targets eg via SEO?
- **Cadence & Personalisation** - What's the right content & when? How do I personalise? What are apps best for?

Expert Recommendation:

- Big Mo's **Web Improvement Grid**: See below.

- **Video Link Examples:** SME Property 1 2 3 4 5 6 7 8 9 10

Big Mo's Web Improvement Grid:

TARGET	Reach	Cadence	Personalise
NEED	SEO improvement based on data analytics	Web/blog improvement via personalisation analysis	App based on personalisation
TOOLS & PARTNERS	Keyword lists & rankings via GTrends Adwords Moz	Web CMS with login or content personalisation tools eg DECCO	App with login eg via Codeless and/or use notifications gateway
FINANCE ANALYSIS	Todays SimpleAI .com	Todays SimpleAI .com	Todays SimpleAI .com
EXAMPLES	Marketing Agencies	Sport/Bet, All Retail, Travel, Finance, B2B, SME, Other	Sport/Bet, All Retail, Travel, Finance, B2B, SME, Other

2.5 The future and future proofing

Trends "as big as the web"...

1. Machine learning.

2. Deep learning..

3. Blockchain for contracts and cryptocurrency.

Only one certainty ... continuous, ever faster change!

So be adaptable to survive and hopefully thrive!

Who proved that first? Darwin wasn't it ... ?

Plus ca change .. plus c'est le meme chose!

A bientot! :)

2.6 Useful Links

My Links:

https://www.linkedin.com/in/mauricebigmoflynn/

https://www.amazon.co.uk/-/e/B078ZGGLCW

Other Links:

https://gdpr-info.eu

https://www.youtube.com/watch?v=KzM-XLwgfAc

https://www.alienvault.com/blogs/security-essentials/a
re-businesses-prepared-for-gdpr

https://vimeo.com/230965114

https://www.youtube.com/watch?v=xIW5RI8K3Yg

https://www.youtube.com/watch?v=Ezdxg4vgAio

https://www.oracle.com/uk/corporate/features/gdpr.html?bcid=5584974298001&playerType=single-social&size=w01&shareUrl=http://www.oracle.com#close

https://vimeo.com/196298299

https://www.youtube.com/watch?v=PToCYQ-cxwk

https://www.youtube.com/watch?v=Vxsu2NMF3vM

https://www.youtube.com/watch?v=PzHZVcWsKvU

https://www.youtube.com/watch?v=1J2rX2Km6Nc

https://www.youtube.com/watch?v=PWa8-43kE-Q&t=16s

https://trends.google.co.uk/trends/

https://adwords.google.com/home/

https://moz.com/tools/rank-tracker

http://www.decco-engine.com

https://www.codelessplatforms.com

https://support.google.com/youtube/answer/6373554?hl=en

https://www.mturk.com

http://wordsmith.readme.io/v1.5/docs

https://www.techsmith.com/jing-tool.html

https://giphy.com

http://webdav.tuebingen.mpg.de/pixel/enhancenet/

https://animoto.com

https://hangouts.google.com

https://support.google.com/youtube/answer/1388383

https://wordpress.org

https://wordpress.com

https://www.youtube.com/watch?v=c1l86Gw8dGo

http://www.trackur.com/quick-start

https://developers.facebook.com/apps

https://www.youtube.com/watch?v=Xwx_Lc_pRsI

Today's AI Artificial Intelligence

Intelligence

It's Not As Difficult As It Sounds!

By Maurice 'Big Mo', Chris & Killian Flynn

Let's Bring the Power
of AI to Everyone!

Today's Simple AI™
TSAI

The FF Foundation is a not-for-profit,

AI research, development & teaching foundation,

currently funded by Open Doors Ltd.

TodaysSimpleAIForAll.eventbrite.com - *TodaysSimpleAI.com*

Any profits from this book will go to charity.
Published 2019 by The FF Foundation & Open Doors Ltd.
Images: Courtesy of Pixabay.com

Index

INDEX

www.ingramcontent.com/pod-product-compliance
Lightning Source LLC
Chambersburg PA
CBHW071418050326
40689CB00010B/1892